ACKNOWLEDGEMENTS

I am most indebted to the six men: Neal Williams, John Berger, David Dean Bottrell, Gerald Chester, John "Allen" Burnett, and Paul Butler, who graciously allowed me to interview them. Their deep insight, wisdom, candor, and occasional humor, was the genesis of this book. I am grateful to members of The West Hollywood Church, and their pastor Rev. Dan Smith, whose lives exhibited for me the meaning of abominable grace. To the members of The Board of Governors of The Lazarus Project I am thankful for the joy of having been a director of that ministry.

I am also indebted to my friend, Dr. Carolyn Shadle, who proofread the manuscript making my punctuation and some of my spelling more orthodox and respectable. The late Rev. Gene Huff read my earliest draft of this book and encouraged me to complete the task.

To the anonymous author of the biographical statement in chapter 1; and to Job Christianson for the inspiration in the development of chapter 7, I am deeply grateful.

In a general sense, in my native Montana, I am indebted to two friends, Rev. Eugene Peterson and Carle O'Neil, both of them authors, who over many years have encouraged me in my writing. And to my brother Ted, a journalist and author, I owe most my love of writing

To my wife Helen, for her forbearance during the years that this book evolved.

CHAPTERS

Preface A Sunday Afternoon - Introductions

Chapter 1   LIFE AS AN ABOMINATION   page 9

Chapter 2   WHO TOOK THE FUN OUT OF   page 25
             FUNDAMENTALISM

Chapter 3   THE FIXERS   page 47

Chapter 4   FAITH OF OUR FATHERS -   page 59
             LIVING STILL

Chapter 5   WHAT'S LOVE GOT TO DO   page 74
             WITH IT?

Chapter 6   THE BIBLE BATTLEMENTS   page 91

Chapter 7   HEARTS OF FLESH   page 110

Chapter 8   THE VANISHING JESUS -   page 128
             " THE UNCARNATION"

Chapter 9   THE DISORIENTED MALE   page 144

Chapter 10 GETTING IT STRAIGHT   page 157

Chapter 11 SEARCHING FOR TEXAS   page 174

Chapter 12 THE GOSPEL AS SONG   page 192

Chapter 13 COMING IN   page 207

Abominable grace is amazing grace
   as seen through the eyes
   of one who resents it,
   as the elder brother resented
   the grace given the prodigal son.

Abominable grace is grace
   another sees as undeserved,
   but then that is what grace always is
   - undeserved.

That is why it is grace.

INTRODUCTION

A Sunday Afternoon

One Sunday afternoon I sat with a group of six men I had asked to interview for this book. I had known each of them for some time and knew something of their stories. What they all had in common, besides being gay, was that they each had come out of a fundamentalist, evangelical, puritan or separatist tradition. Here and there I would ask a question to move the discussion to certain aspects of their experience, but little priming was necessary as they had remarkable stories to tell and the capacity to tell them in an extraordinary way. Each of these men had come back to the Church through a long and difficult journey. What I cannot begin to capture in these pages is the ambiance of that day - the abundant laughter, the joy that they had come to out of painful experiences, the depth and vitality of their faith.

Since they are often quoted in this book I will introduce you to them here. We met in the hone of **John** and **Neal** who have been together for more than twenty years. They are married. Although there is currently a stay on same sex marriages in California pending the outcome of an appeal to the California Supreme Court, they were married during the brief window of opportunity when that was legal, and those marriages remain valid.

The living room where we gathered, as the rest of the house, reflects their life together and their considerable creativity. More than a house, it is a home, and a place of warmth and abundant hospitality. Both are attorneys. Neal received his undergraduate degree from Wheaton College and John from Westmont, both evangelical colleges. They met at a gay Bible study. John is a strong competitor in a gay tennis league, and Neal has done some turns as a standup comic.

Gerald is also an attorney. He and his partner, Santiago, also have been together for over twenty years. Gerald grew up in The Church of Christ. He taught English in a conservative Christian college before studying law at Loyola.

Paul, who studied at The Bible Institute of Los Angeles (BIOLA) has had a varied career. He worked many years in law enforcement and was the first LAPD officer to come out while on the force. He, too, has worked in standup comedy. He is currently the Director of Security of the museums of a major university. He is also a painter.

David, a successful screenwriter and actor, is the son of a Pentecostal minister. He grew up in a series of small towns in Kentucky and Southern Ohio. Although he is primarily known as a comedy writer, the majority of the films he has written contain underlying spiritual or redemptive themes. David recently helped create a program to mentor young gay and lesbian writers.

Allen, who is African-American, grew up in a small coal mining town in West Virginia and sometimes refers to himself as "a coalminer's daughter." A retired audiologist, Allen is an Air Force veteran. For many years he has sung with the Gay Men's Chorus of Los Angeles and recently toured with them in Russia and eastern Europe.

In 1995 I began what became for me a journey in which I entered a world I knew about but that was largely not my world. Since then it has become a significant part of my life and of the world I live in. I expected to do a job, one that challenged me and about which I had deep conviction. I had not anticipated how greatly I would be affected by the lives of those with whom I began to journey.

I took my formal retirement as a Presbyterian minister and accepted a part-time position as Director of The Lazarus Project, a largely educational and advocacy ministry whose mission was to try and move the Presbyterian Church in Southern California to become more welcoming of gay and lesbian persons. I set up an office in our home in the picturesque, New Englandish college town of Claremont (think of Vermont without snow and with occasional palm trees). The ivy league mentality is palpable in our two street - Harvard and Yale - village shopping area, adjacent to the five Claremont Colleges, Graduate School, and School of Theology. I would, however, spend at least one day a week at the official Lazarus office located on Sunset Boulevard in The West Hollywood Presbyterian Church, 42 miles west and a hemisphere away from Claremont.

West Hollywood, with large populations of gays and Russian Jewish immigrants (populations not to be confused with each other), and Claremont are vastly different environments. I began to have a kind of bicultural existence. "Women are from Venus, Men are from Mars," however in West Hollywood it would not be too difficult to find some men who are from Venus, and women who are from Mars. Though neither urban environments nor the gay community were foreign to me, the up-close observation of the lives of these persons generated within me some intense theological reflection, a reexamination of my faith and my view of the Church. For the first several months after I began with the Lazarus Project I visited other congregations on Sunday mornings trying to raise the visibility of our ministry by being present and introducing myself to the pastor, and to others, during the customary social time following the service. It had been over thirty years since I had been the person in the pew rather than in the chancel or the pulpit. Through those years I sat facing those in the pews; now I was one of them. It was a new and, in many ways, a troubling perspective. Much of the problem was my own expanded view which made me even more aware than I had been of the not only entrenched, but aggressive conservatism among many in my denomination. And I knew that what I saw was generally true in most other mainline denominations.

Over the years, Christian fundamentalism had bled through to the so-called mainline denominations through those who designated themselves as evangelicals, an identity that seemed more primary to them than any denominational affiliation. This has been especially true in Southern California. While many who call themselves evangelicals want to distinguish between themselves and fundamentalists, the distinction has sometimes been difficult to find.

During my years in ministry, I had not been living a sheltered denominational life. The small but progressive congregation that I served for twenty years had already been engaged in our denomination's ongoing holy war over the ordination of openly gay and lesbian persons. Following my retirement I more and more began worshiping at the West Hollywood Presbyterian Church even though it entailed more than an hour's drive. At that time my impression of it was that this small congregation had a kind of "Biblical look" just in its human diversity, sort of like the crowds that gathered around Jesus. There were young professionals, and some retired persons, and occasional homeless individuals. Many were outsiders, if not outcasts, of the wider society and especially of the Church. This small congregation was very much the exception rather than the rule in the denomination.

Though it has since become more gender diversified, when I began attending West Hollywood the congregation was very predominantly men (in reverse of most Presbyterian congregations where there is a predominance of women). For its size there was a real rather than token integration of African-Americans, Hispanics, and Asians. But in one way the congregation at that time was near monolithic. Almost everyone in it was gay or lesbian.*

The first few Sundays I was there I would find myself deeply affected not so much by any particular part of the liturgy, the sermon, or the music, as by the congregation itself. Never had the words of worship seemed so deeply related to those who heard them and spoke them. I was moved simply by being among this particular people of God. The situation gave an incredible authenticity to the content of worship. You felt like you were worshiping in the catacombs. I learned that to worship with oppressed persons is to journey in the company of those whose life together becomes in itself an exposition of the Gospel.

These persons, like others, had much going on in their lives that did not revolve around their being gay, and my awareness of them as oppressed persons was not necessarily their own focus. Even so, though they did not present themselves as victims, neither were they at all unaware of their situation in the society-at-large. There were sometimes deeply painful reminders such as the murder of Matthew Shepherd, the AIDS epidemic, "Don't Ask, Don't Tell," and one evening on a street in West Hollywood the beating into a coma with a baseball bat of a young man who was saying goodnight to a friend.

I thought about how Jews had been "a light to the Gentiles" not because of any moral superiority but because of circumstances - journeys, as I have mentioned - through which they evolved toward a unique God-consciousness. In their journeying, they experienced an extraordinary dependence on God's leading and God's providing. During and after Biblical times through their experiences of being cast out, exiled, and ghettoized, they became a light, an instrument of revelation. Gays, having similar experiences of oppression, have broken the darkness in a similar way. That is not a claim I make for them of moral superiority but only a confession that, for me at least, and I believe for many others, their circumstances lead one to an awareness of God that does not come with such clarity in the midst of the everyday, and in the company of the mainstream. The Roman Catholic priest and theologian, Henri Nouwen, described a similar experience in choosing during the later years of his life to leave the rarefied atmosphere of Harvard to live and serve among the mentality handicapped in the L'Arche community in Toronto.

There is a story, perhaps apocryphal, that someone once asked Mrs. Alfred Kinsey, "How is your husband?" She replied, "I don't know really, I scarcely see him since he became interested in sex." Sex is rather compelling subject matter as it leads into so many aspects of human behavior and relationships.

One of the great hazards in writing this book, which I realized from the beginning, is that since it is about homosexuals, many people may think it is a book about sex. However, one of the objectives of this book is to show that the over association of those who are called homosexuals with sex is central to the hugely distorted way in which many see them. Where this book, out of some necessity, does address issues of human sexuality, it is for the purpose of addressing that fixation that many have regarding gay persons, in order to move beyond it. Sexuality is a part, a significant part, of gay persons lives, as it is a significant part of the lives of others, but the hope here is that gays may be seen and understood more wholistically than has often been the case.

The ministry in which I was engaged was not to change minds that are made up and essentially closed, which are many, but, if possible, to reach those hearts, and minds, that are still open. They may be open simply because they love someone who is gay, a family member or friend, and love wants to find a way toward understanding. This book is written for them, especially if their obstacle toward understanding is their religious orientation. It is written for parents, grandparents, siblings and friends who love persons who are gay but feel unsure how to express and practice that love toward them. This is also written for gays who love the Church but who find the Church does not love them, and who find it increasingly difficult to stay where they feel they are not wanted, or know that they will not in the present be treated justly. And it is written for those gays who understandably have given up on the Church but still hold the Gospel in their hearts. Hopefully this book may even be useful to some straight persons in the Church who honestly struggle to understand why gays do not accept what seems so clearly to them to be the truth. In summary, this is written for any who truly want to enlarge their understanding both of gays and of the Gospel.

  I write as a pastor and an advocate, not as an academic. I write about persons who are abused in this society, and yes, I try to identify their abusers, especially those who use religion as a defense. I have also tried very hard to understand the origins of their inclination to demonize gay persons. I had also to know my limits in terms of what I felt qualified to write. I knew enough of the stories and experience of lesbian women to know that is not simply the flip side of gay male experience. Theirs is a somewhat different phenomena and I believe it takes a woman to describe that phenomena. Transgender experience requires an expertise of its own, possessed most by those who are transgendered, and there are far more of those I believe than the general public is aware.

  What I have endeavored to do over these last several years is to know deeply gay and lesbian persons; to honor their struggle, celebrate their lives, enjoy their grace and humor, and respect their spirituality. In knowing them this has required no effort at all. What would have required effort, and rationalization, would have been to feel any other way. I have also tried to understand theologically why their lives are such an extraordinary problem for a variety of Christians and other persons. That has required considerable effort and I have come, I'm sure, only part of the distance toward that understanding.

A note of explanation seems necessary regarding inclusive language. Because of deficiencies in the English language itself there were some unavoidable choices to be made between sensitivity to gender issues, and style. Since I care about both, these were often difficult choices. There are several omissions in the language that create this problem. One is that we do not have a personal ungendered pronoun in the third person singular. I am often talking about the Church; and to call the Church "it," to avoid the gendered pronouns of "he" or "she," particularly in some contexts, robs something from the meaning of that human institution. Another great problem in speaking of God is the lack of any non-gendered personal form of mother/father. "Parent,"' or even "loving parent," is too formal and carries little of the deep feeling content of father or mother. Though God is not male nor female, that felt relationship of ourselves as children of God is essential to much of what is written here. In various instances throughout the book I simply do my best to convey that relationship and when I can, to also dissociate God from the gender stereotypes of both father and mother. There is no perfect solution, so I must simply ask the reader's forbearance in this matter.

*Since my original writing of this book The West Hollywood Presbyterian Church, wearied from the glacial pace of change in the PCUSA, has left the denomination for the more inclusive United Church of Christ.

Chapter 1

Life As An Abomination

"And then Anita Bryant - the orange juice lady - came on the scene...and was getting a lot of press about how we all had to band together to protect our communities from these pushy homosexuals. Well, that suddenly inspired the minister of our local church to take up the cause, and he began preaching about how homosexuality was an abomination in the eyes of God, and he made it clear that the whole subject was so disgusting he could barely talk about it. I wasn't even sure exactly what he was talking about, but clearly whatever it was - it was so revolting that any discussion of it would make people vomit in the aisles."
David

Many children, perhaps more than ten per cent, grow up in our society with a dawning awareness of something about themselves which they instinctively realize they must hide from any other human being - their parents, their siblings, their friends, their teachers - everyone. For some of them "the terrible secret" is like a bomb strapped to their body, with the constant fear that something may trigger it and it will go off and destroy them. They sense, though they cannot understand, that there is something different about them that may be potentially repugnant to others, including their parents. For some of these children this instinctive knowledge comes even before they enter the first grade. It tends to come sooner for boys than for girls because the norms of the culture set it in higher relief. They feel shame and potential alienation, often without understanding why, but knowing intuitively that they dare not ask - anyone.

The taunts of schoolyard bullies, even when not directed at them, often sent them the first chilling message of their "queerness." Puberty arrived and knowledge informed instinct. They began to know why, and how, they were "queer," discovering that they were more attracted emotionally, and therefore sexually, to their own gender than to the opposite one. They found themselves out of sync with the cultural norms of their gender. "Gender nonconformity" some will name it, their nicety for "queer."

Sixty years ago, the second world war had just begun. I was 12, in grade seven, not a very popular kid, picked on a lot, hated it. I knew some guys I liked but they seemed too aloof. There was no response as friends. I was frozen out. I didn't excel at much, at least hadn't yet learned I could. Sort of lonely, a dreamer, romantic, I needed affirmation by more than my dog. But not fully understanding needs, I was aware of growing, of newly sprouting erotic feelings. Leading where? After school one day an older boy invited himself over, and WOW, sparks flew, emotions overflowed, new worlds blossomed. Sex became a reality. Who could have imagined? It was so neat, so natural, exciting, but oh so secret The next day at school some older boys looked down at me, laughed tauntingly. Now what was happening? I thought back. On the defensive again. Damn! One of them opened his mouth, put his lips over his teeth, "Hey kid, let's see how you do this. Come on homo, show us how you do it, homo." What the hell is a "homo?" Where the hell are they coming from? I had a new name to be beat up with. Such was an 'outing' 60 years ago....no word for it. One blissful encounter becomes an unexpected, misunderstood moment of self-revelation.

Such was the discovery of my same-sex attraction and my encounter with a world of fear, intimidation, hatred and bigotry. Being outed as a gay (no such word then) kid

60 years ago, on the threshold of puberty, made one the perfect victim. You couldn't escape, ask for help or protection, or discuss your feelings. There was no one you could talk to, for every search for help you just knew would turn against you. All you could do was try to survive.

Three years later at the end of grade nine, after a lot of bad times, mingled with some really good moments, we moved 2000 miles away. So began 45 years of living in the closet. No way in hell would I tell anyone of my same sex attraction. It was a chance to start anew, without an unchosen label, a detested category, a chance to escape, to find part of the me that no one would ever have accepted in the old community. What a relief, a new world. Then followed the years of trying to reconcile the tensions within; with all normal activities of a young man in pursuit of self-discovery: dating girls, love affairs, education, work, contact sports, military and war. Yet, continually lurking in the shadows was same sex attraction. Deny it, suppress it, pray it away, ignore it, fear it, - want it. God, what a hostile world: gay death in the holocaust, gays treated as criminals, not victims, Senator McCarthy and J. Edgar Hoover's witch hunts, religious blindness and bigotry, police repression and harassment. Who wanted to confront such a world. Hide! Deny! Stay safe.

Yet, there did come a time. The world had changed somewhat. Immersion in the Black Civil Right Movement, the quest for women's' freedom and third world liberation set precedents and empowered. So 45 years later 'out' I came, with a supportive wife, into this different world where now there were some safe places not only to be oneself but to celebrate the fact. Too late in life to relive the past, but time enough to watch with joy the emerging freedom of the young, to take part in consolidating the gains, even savor the erotic. Yet, still, the lessons from my past breed caution, for there lurks in all of us an incipient intolerance toward difference, that, like the spark of tinder under the right conditions, can start again the flames of violence and hatred.

As, among other things, an ordained Christian clergy person, I find one of the most virulent types to fear are Christian fundamentalists who misuse scripture to justify their prejudices. The result is their complicity in maintaining the violence and hatred to which same sex oriented persons are subjected. They present an image of Christianity warped from a religion of love and freedom, to one of oppression, narrow prejudice and particularism. The Biblical theology they pursue is the same one that led them to support slavery, dehumanize other races, religions and cultures, and oppress women. And, as in the past, they do it in almost total ignorance of those whom they choose to demonize.

*Anony*mous

A common characteristic, though not a universal one, of gay boys is that they are "the best little boys in whole wide world." That syndrome represents perhaps an inward perception that they need to be that "perfect child" to store up grace with their parents so that if they are ever discovered to be gay, their parents will still have to love them. In a small town, for parents to have a gay child was to have one who was thought to be abnormal - "queer" - not in the biological sense but in the moral sense. Because deep shame was attached to that for the parent as well as the child, parents tended to be in denial of any evidence they did not want to see. From that the child easily got the message that he or she was potentially a source of shame or embarrassment to their parents and would compensate by trying to be the exemplary child.

The closet was the only refuge for those who risked being called "queer," "homo," "sissy," "fairy" or "fag." For a child or youth who was beginning to perceive that they were gay a terrifying message was sent just by there not even being a word for such persons that wasn't negative, mean, and excluding. "Homosexuals" was a term pretty much left to clinicians. You can imagine the place persons would have in a society that had nothing but contemptuous, hateful, and derisive words for them.

Since life as an abomination is no picnic, many of the best little boys in the whole wide world have tried everything in the whole wide world to de-abominate themselves. There have always been others around to prescribe how this might be accomplished: fervent prayer, counseling, sports, self-discipline, fasting, electroshock therapy - and if all else fails - castration. The Los Angeles Times recently carried a brief news item about a Taiwanese man who claims to have castrated about fifty people. He may not, however, have committed any crime according to police in the Detroit suburb of Oak Park, because the castrations were requested by consenting adults. Officers said the unlicensed surgeon apparently was contacted through Web sites promoting castration. No one was sure why persons would request this but an educated guess would be that many of them were gay men.

David was the first to venture forth when I asked the six men gathered in John and Neal's living room, *"What religious or spiritual experience do you identify as being related to your sexuality?"*

"Well, I've been known to cry out God's name every once in a while!" David, a storyteller, has the gift to lead with humor and then take one to a deeper level. As the laughter subsides he continues; *"There was never any discussion of sex, period, anywhere around church, and my parents were very religious people, so there was no discussion of sex in our house, ever! No one ever said, 'Let me sit down and talk with you about the facts of life.'*

My mother knocked on my bedroom door one day and I opened it, and she handed me a book called 'Ann Landers Talks to Teenagers About Sex.' And she said,

"Here, read this." And that was it. So I did read 'Ann Landers Talks to Teens,' and there was only one reference to homosexuality in it, and basically all Ann had to say was, "Don't worry, it's just a phase, it's just a little crush. It will go away." So I held onto that for a long time hoping that Ann was right. Except my phase didn't seem to go away. It actually got worse. And then Anita Bryant - the orange juice lady - came on the scene...., It was inferred that homosexuals recruited children from churches and schoolyards and converted them while they were still young and impressionable.

Well, each Sunday, I started sinking a little lower in my pew trying to be as invisible as I could be since I was pretty sure that I was turning into one of these creepy, horrible people. It was the beginning of my trying to fight my feelings. And it was a long fight. I tried several times to have relationships with women in college, but none of them worked out for obvious reasons.

Anyway, I fought it, and fought it, and fought it, until I couldn't fight it any more. When I came out, I just gave up on the whole God package. I just rejected it -- threw it out of my life. I developed this really hostile attitude about the church and felt sort of proud that I didn't need God anymore. But the truth is I was very hurt. Down deep, I felt like an orphan who'd been kicked out on the street. It was incredibly scary at first. Now, when I think about how alone I was as a teenager - how much I felt like a freak - it kills me. All those years hating my own guts, and feeling so separate from the whole. I'm sure I've put a new wing on my therapist's house talking about this subject. But with nobody to help you, you can wind up with all these layers of self-loathing, some of them very subtle. I think I've done a pretty good job cleaning up that mess, but every once in a while something will happen and I'll discover another layer I didn't even know was there.

Gerald

I didn't get Ann Landers but I got Pat Boone. It's still amazing how it was communicated to me. I know my parents were concerned when I was in high school that I didn't date. They didn't like any of my school friends and felt I should associate with people from my church. Late in high school I was dating this woman but I was about to be shipped off to this rural place where they wanted me to go, a Christian college in Texas. I got to Abilene and in the second year there two guys in the dorm were petting and got expelled from school. I remember that but I don't remember having much reaction to it because I think during all that time I was sexless. There was sex going on; I was intrigued, but I kept my distance.

I left that environment and went to a state university - another culture shock. I was experiencing a warp in my sexuality. I don't know how I knew from the beginning....how the church of my youth communicated this taboo. In the university community you learn about a lot of things, so I kind of developed an awareness.

After I graduated, I started teaching at a Christian college and I knew that my physical attraction was for men, and I confided in the dean of the school and he suggested I go to New York or San Francisco.

With the exception of a few very strange folks out there, like those who demonstrated at Matthew Shepherd's funeral, no one claiming to represent the Church would use street or schoolyard language like "queer, fairy, sissy, homo, and fag." They have a more Biblical word. They simply call them, or "it," an abomination. (Many choose to assume that "them" and "it," the person and the act, are separable). God, of course, does not make abominations so how did they get to be one? The Church's answer, much of it, has been - they chose it. Their impression seems to be that some very nice young boy is growing up, going to Sunday School, doing his homework, playing soccer, and then - bam, one day he decides that instead of dating girls and going to the prom, he'll become a loathsome homosexual, an abomination in his parents and everyone else's eyes. Who knew that such a seemingly nice young boy had such an evil heart?

The idea that homosexuals choose their sexual orientation, as almost every gay person on the planet would tell you, is irrational and absurd. But who is listening?

I'm not sure why we are gay. Of course there are a number of theories about that. I've had cousins say to me, "Why do you do this?" and "You know your hurting your relatives," or something like that. It's not something I have a choice in and I try to explain. I wish people understood that one fact about us.

Allen

For many Christians, and other folks, it just seems there can be no other explanation than that gays choose their sexual orientation. Their point of view is that their God would not make homosexuals, so what other explanation could there be? The general attitude is, they chose it and they - with God's help of course - can change it. And even if they didn't choose it, or can't change it, they can be chaste - which means to them - celibate.

To hold a conviction, one way or the other, about something beyond the realm of demonstrable proof may be identified as belief. But to hold a conviction that something is true (i.e. that sexual orientation is chosen) though the great preponderance of observable, verifiable evidence indicates it is not true, is not simply to hold a contrary belief, it is to be in denial. If an adult were to say that he or she believes in Santa Claus, and not as an allegorical figure but as a real person who resides at the North Pole, that would not really be belief, it would be denial. It is the denial of some reality the individual does not want to accept. The convictions that many hold about gay persons are not so much a product of their belief as of their denial.

What is the most significant evidence, and testimony, as to whether or not something is true, evidence that in itself is not proof but provides the most significant data? It obviously is the witness of those whose experience is in question. That is the primary empirical data. The persons who have the right to say, and the ability to know, whether or not they chose their sexual orientation are those persons whose sexual orientation is the object of the discussion. No one who is not gay has the right to say, because it is what they want to believe, that a homosexual orientation is chosen. They can speak with authority only as to whether or not they chose their own. And when asked to speak to that which they are in the better position to know, they will usually acknowledge that they have no awareness of having chosen their own sexual orientation. In fact, they would often be reluctant to even consider such a thought for fear it might imply they are actually bisexual.

Largely associated with Roman Catholic priests and nuns celibacy is not something of which Protestants have been great advocates apart from this issue. There is considerable disagreement in the Church as to whether chastity means being celibate. The Heidelberg Catechism says that married persons should be chaste, which would imply the meaning of chastity is faithfulness. But, of course, for those who reject the validity of committed relationships between same sex couples, faithfulness is irrelevant and, other than heterosexual marriage (which isn't really heterosexual marriage if one of the persons in it is not heterosexual), celibacy seems to them the only moral alternative for gay persons.

Most conservatives believe the meaning of being chaste is that single persons (which for them includes even homosexual persons in committed relationships) should be celibate. It is rather amazing that celibacy now seems such a good idea, and possible, for many persons who expect their spouses to respond to their "needs" on a regular basis. In some instances, of course, individuals may feel that their own sex lives are unsatisfactory to non existent so it doesn't seem unfair if such expectations are put on others. What doesn't get much acknowledgement is that gay persons who love one another are as inclined as heterosexual persons to express that in lovemaking.

The Church's insistence on celibacy for single persons, or persons they insist on defining as single, is one that exists largely for rhetorical purposes but seems not to have been thought out at a personal level. I found myself one day in conversation with a young minister regarding gays in the Church, a discussion that was going nowhere except stirring up his emotions and mine. So rather than continue to debate theological issues and zing Bible verses at each other, I asked him if he was a father. He said that he was. I said, "I am a father too, and though my child is not gay, if he were, I think I'd feel a special concern for him. I wonder if your child were to grow up and one day tell you that he is gay, would you really want him to commit himself to being celibate all of his life, to live a lonely life - for it would be - and never experience physical intimacy with another person? Is that what, as a father, you would want for your child?" He was quiet for a moment and then he said, "No, it isn't." I was moved by his honesty, though he probably still held out hope that a gay child could become "straight."

I had asked the group if there had been a point where they felt their religious orientation and their sexual orientation collided. John told of how even a small evangelical Christian college (Westmont) did not keep someone from knocking on his closet door. It was a frightening experience:

> *I became friends with a group of people who were Pentecostal, and I didn't know what that meant. But the thing about it was we all became friends. We all became really good friends and I could be friends with guys in a different way than ever before because they all hugged each other, which I thought was really odd, but I liked it. I can't say why I liked it, but I did. One guy used to call me brother. I had an incredible crush on him and it was okay because we were in a Christian group where we hugged each other. So it was a kind of cover. You could date girls but you didn't have to do anything with them because you were always saving yourself, and it wasn't the Christian thing to do.*
>
> *Where it collided for me was I met this guy at college, and we were best friends. In my junior year we were going to become roommates. He took me up to the library because he said he had something to tell me. And I thought, "What could this be?" We went on the balcony and he said, "Before we become roommates next year I have to tell you something." And I said, "What is it?'" and he said, "I'm homosexual." And I said, "No you're not!" and he said, "Yes, I am." "I said, "No, you can't be, that's impossible!"*
>
> *It frightened me. I was beyond scared for a couple of reasons: I was a Christian and I couldn't understand how you could be Christian and gay. I was extremely close to him and really loved him, and thought "Oh My God, he felt that way about me. We've been hugging all the time and when we become roommates..."'" The other thing was he was pretty 'out,' meaning he didn't care if people knew and in a small school like Westmont if I was going to be his roommate that would be the end of me as well. So I left the balcony and I never talked to him again. I went way back in*

the closet. I didn't talk to him for the rest of my junior year and my senior year. Our friendship ended by that conversation on the balcony.

"Did he try to talk to you?" I asked.

Yes, but I didn't want to be around him anymore. Years later....many, many years later, after Neal and I were together, we were in San Francisco and we ran into him at a park, and I asked him to forgive me. I knew it was a terrible thing. He said he knew it really bugged me. I really regret that I treated him so poorly, but I was afraid. I couldn't put the two together....the gay and the Christian...

I've always been somewhat amazed, given how homophobic this society has been, that ordinary persons could easily accept "queerness" in the form of popular entertainment. The old traditional view of gay men was that they had high voices, limp wrists, would lisp, and that they were effeminate and flamboyant. Though that was often treated with abhorrence, if you put it on a stage in Las Vegas, midwestern wives would line up and pay to see it, and their husbands would go along quite willingly. In such a homophobic culture I was always amazed at the success of Liberace. All sorts of women and men loved not only his music but his audacity. Did they not think he was gay? Though much of his life he denied being gay, as most gay artists do because they do not want to be exclusively identified as a gay performer, he nonetheless was a flaming queen almost without peer. In a way it was a remarkable triumph.

Today the demeanor of many gay men is strongly in the other direction. Many of them have become "super masculine." That is no doubt reactive. Some of them perhaps as children read the "Mr. Atlas" advertisements and decided that instead of being the scrawny guy who gets sand kicked in his face they would become Mr. Atlas.

In what is called "Boys' Town," at one end of Santa Monica Boulevard in West Hollywood one might make a relatively safe guess that a man with a conspicuously superior physique is gay. However, even those with less than spectacular hard bodies do not usually fit the old limp wrist stereotype. In most instances you would not be likely to "know one when you see one." Apart from the subculture of hard bodies, age and lifestyle tend to effect the bodies of gay and straight men in the same way, and most gay men, as most straight men, are not centerfold material. Effeminacy, except sometimes as a "put on," is not characteristic of most gay men.

In recent years the objections of many have been not so much about persons being gay as to their "coming out." It is the assertion of gay pride, the demand for gay rights, that gets people excited. The attitude seems to be like this: *"Things were working fine. We were willing to leave them alone. A certain accommodation could be made. Why couldn't they leave things as they were? Now they're holding hands where we can see them, even kissing in public. They flaunt it. Only we who are straight are entitled to do that."*

One particular problem the gay community in the Church faces is that if people can't get them for what they say, they will try to get them for how they say it. If gays call attention to their abuse, they will be accused of exploiting themselves as victims; if they show their outrage, they will be dismissed as too aggressive; if they organize, they will be criticized for having a "gay agenda." When gays push for action and change, they are reminded that change takes time and that they must have patience and forbearance, or they are charged with being "single issue." (It is endemic to oppression that it tends to make persons, if not "single issue" at least intent upon seeking freedom from that oppression). Seeking equal rights and protection against discrimination, they are often accused of seeking "special rights." If they talk openly about their lives and relationships or show the signs of affection that heterosexuals take for granted, they are accused of flaunting themselves. And if they present thoughtful and careful exegesis (analysis, interpretation) of scriptural passages, including those often used to condemn them, they will be branded out of hand as not "Bible believing," and as secularists who have sold out their faith for a "social gospel." There are conservatives, and sometimes moderates, stationed on every road endeavoring to keep them from going anywhere.

The fear is that if persons can "come out," they can and will then press for a different social order, one that does not discriminate against them. Straights love to speak in sinister tones about "the gay agenda," as if they have none and as if it would be subversive for gays to want to end the socially sanctioned abuses against them. Boiled down, the "gay agenda" is the one that tends to belong to every individual or group of oppressed persons - "justice!" And that is the one that scares people. Justice doesn't mean a little tolerance here and there; it means substantive, structural change.

Equality, and thereby justice, is always about the distribution, or redistribution, of power. For the under empowered to achieve equality the over empowered must always give up some of their power, either willingly or unwillingly. There is, however, in that shift of power a new kind of empowerment even for those reluctant to let go, the power of love, the power inherent to persons living in a just society. But initially that tends not to be seen nor greatly valued by those who feel power is being taken away from them.

In this society, although less so now than in the past, to be heterosexual as opposed to homosexual, to be straight rather than gay, is to be empowered. To be Caucasian is to belong to an empowered minority. Wealth amplifies the power even of someone in a minority; to have resources or access to resources amplifies power.

It amazes me that "justice" is such a big word in scripture and such a small word in the Church. Those on one side virtually never use it, as though it were extraneous to the Gospel or even subversive. In an article in one of the newsletters that comes from the conservative wing of our denomination the writer was alerting the readers of signs to watch for in candidates for ministry. One of these was that if a candidate used the word "justice" in his or her examination for ordination; be aware, they are probably "liberal."

"Justice," they suspect, is a "liberal" word more than a biblical one, a leftist word, an excuse for permissiveness, a "bleeding heart" word. How interesting that "bleeding heart" should be used by conservative Christians as a term of derision against others, though what "bleeding heart" most describes is Jesus. Who is more likely to talk about the blood of Jesus being shed for others than fundamentalists?

Many Christians wanting to show tolerance toward gays will say that homosexuality is just a sin like any other. But in reality it is almost always treated as a sin like no other. Many of the persons who do that seem to have no awareness of it, or if they do see it, are unable to offer any real explanation as to why the extraordinary reaction. Why is homosexuality treated differently than other "sins" by those who insist it is sin? Perhaps it is because, unlike other behaviors, what is perceived even if unarticulated - and the perception is correct - is that if attitudes about homosexuality change, there will follow from that a systemic change in the social order. That is now happening over the issue of gay marriage, a prospect which terrifies many conservatives.

Justice, which lies in balance, always involves a shift in power away from the over empowered toward the under empowered and disempowered. Empowered majorities fear that. They tend to favor charity over justice because charity maintains the hierarchical order, is basically condescending, whereas justice seeks a more horizontal and egalitarian structure.

Justice is the agenda, if one is to speak of an agenda, but the effect of justice replacing injustice is inevitably structural change. It is that change that is passionately resisted. What many fear is the renouncing of heterosexual privilege and supremacy, and the real fall of heterosexism. What is not seen by those who resist is that what they so greatly fear will in its coming only enrich their world and their lives.

Chapter 2

Who Took the Fun
out of Fundamentalism

"I have been seized by the power of a great affection."
Creole expression for "saved"

There was fun in fundamentalism. Good times. Fun of course doesn't really describe it. It was something more than that, something deeper. It was joy. And it broke in on people living hard, and often turbulent lives. They were seized by the power of a great affection. That is why it is so remembered, and so difficult for many to leave any part of it behind. Unlike the religious practice of many, it was not just a part, not just occasional, but the very matrix of their lives. A whole congregation very often was a kind of extended family. It wasn't always a healthy family for everyone in it but even dysfunctional families sometimes have great moments. People were alive, clapping their hands, saying "amen," sometimes literally jumping with joy. It was a natural high, and often addictive. There was the continual drama of peoples' lives revealed in testimonies and altar calls. Better than TV, they were like living books. (Despite the dark side of it, no film has probably done a better job of capturing this than Robert Duval's "The Apostle.") And it felt safe. "A shelter in the time of storm," and there was plenty of storm in the world and perhaps in their own lives.

But the good times ended for some, and often bitterly for gays. And it was anything but safe for them. They were cast out of the family, or burdened with shame too heavy to bear. The Gospel turned on them. Their dancing turned to dancing in the flames.

When I was an adolescent, fundamentalists, though they seemed to me outwardly anti-sexual, were paradoxically, I thought, rather sensual, more than what one was apt to find in many of the staid mainline churches. Around my high school the young women of their congregations were easily identified as the ones without lipstick. I've always thought that Tammy Faye Bakker was the revenge of the girls who were forbidden to wear makeup. Ironically their bare lips made them seem somewhat "naked" and alluring.

Despite their apparent antisexual attitudes, there was much in the emotional exuberance of these fundamentalists that seemed to be a kind of sublimated sexuality (though there are forms of fundamentalism that are characterized more by their austerity than by visual displays of emotion). The down side with those who practice such exuberance is that they tend to be less demanding that their faith have some confluence with reason. In that regard there are almost no correctives for their theological improvisations. Feelings are everything.

Sexuality seemed to lie barely below the surface of some prayer meetings. Where the Spirit is so aroused, the flesh may not be altogether disengaged. Praying with others had a profound kind of intimacy to it, especially when kneeling. There is a sort of surrender in that act which verges on the erotic. Praise services provide a "safe" environment for many men, who tending to be more repressed emotionally than women give reign to their emotions. And interestingly this emotion is expressed as love for a man, Jesus Christ.

Though some may doubt, want to invalidate, or choose not to believe that many gay and lesbian persons "have been seized by the power of a great affection," the fact is they have. The somewhat unique problem gays encounter is that often they are deprived of the opportunity to share that experience in the community of the Church.

This book is in large part about the religious experience of gay men. When the religious environment in which they have grown up is Christian fundamentalism, they are likely to have a more difficult road toward self-acceptance. Though I have much to say here about fundamentalism, I am not speaking about all Christian fundamentalism, nor all fundamentalists. I want to make careful distinctions and not do as is often done to gays, lump everyone together within one category and define them by the characteristics and behavior of a few.

Though it is lessening in some ways, and in some places, gays experience what can only be described as oppression. That is the reality that must be named: oppression, injustice, and abuse. Those terms should not be hushed nor softened for the comfort of those they offend. The refusal by many to acknowledge this reality, and their own complicity in it, is part of the oppression itself. Matthew Shepherd was literally crucified in rural America at the close of the twentieth century for being gay. Though he was only mortal, his death offers some of the same revelation as is in the crucifixion of Jesus; evil is revealed as evil, and besides the actual executioners, are the many who, even if unknowingly, created them.

Christian fundamentalism is where much of the abuse of gays originates, though I trust the reader will understand I do not see all who may fit theologically under that heading as being the same in their attitudes or treatment of gays. Not all who would designate themselves as fundamentalists fall inevitably into these patterns, and not all fundamentalist preachers lead them there. There are

African-American fundamentalist churches which are not only sensitive to but activist in working against prejudice and discrimination. The Metropolitan Community Churches, a gay denomination founded by Rev. Troy Perry, a former Pentecostal minister, has roots that are fundamentalist. One of the grassroots organizations for gay and lesbian Christians, Evangelicals Concerned, was begun by an evangelical "Christian" psychotherapist. Mel White, founder of "Soul Force," an ecumenical coalition to move the Church toward inclusiveness related to sexual orientation, came directly out of the fundamentalist community and was once the ghost writer for the biographies of two of its most visible anti-gay protagonists, Pat Robertson and Jerry Falwell.

Jesus had much to say about shepherds and sheep. In parable, he spoke with great compassion for the sheep and was sharply critical of the shepherd who leads his flock astray. Jesus identifies himself as the good shepherd. My concern is not about the sheep so much as it is about the shepherds, often false shepherds, and shepherds in sheep's clothing. What motivates them? Some may simply be crass materialists, others find power and fame seductive. Those infections of course do not happen just to fundamentalists. Some perhaps are driven by personal demons. Some may be simply motivated by a want of security and good feeling.

The true common ground for Christians, including those who are thought of as "liberal," or who think of themselves as "progressives," is in the sharing of the religious experience. Many Christian fundamentalists seem to believe that the faith experience of those who are more liberal in their theology, or whose form of worship is more formal, have less authentic experience than their own. Under the banner of evangelism they want to plant a flag on the Church invisible and claim it as their's alone. But that is simply naked imperialism.

Central perhaps to all fundamentalists is their experience of being "born again." This is now so embedded in the culture that much of the media, wrongly and naively, regularly categorizes Christians in America as being "Born Again" or "Mainline," as though those are mutually exclusive categories. Fundamentalists have successfully co-opted the media to make a distinction that does not exist. Millions who belong to "mainline" denominations attest also to being "born again." But to those who pirate that term it usually means to them that they are "real" as opposed to merely "professing" Christians.

For them there are several, and sometimes many doctrines that are the only ones consistent with that experience. These are the "fundamentals" to which they adhere. They are usually taught to them by whatever pastor or charismatic leader has been to them the agent of their "born again" experience. From that the leader gains acceptance as an authority figure, and in turn the believer gains a sense of assurance - "Blessed Assurance" - that Jesus is theirs, and that they have the proper beliefs to "sustain" their salvation. The charismatic leader often has a hook to hold them - fear. If they veer from his or her version of the gospel they risk eternal damnation. The fundamentalist preacher, who perhaps lives under the same fear, declares that the threat comes not from him but from God, and who can hide from God?

What can easily happen is that existing prejudice becomes incorporated into the "fundamentals," and the drive to evangelize becomes the opportunity to export those same prejudices. The nature of prejudice is that it makes persons feel secure within their "tribe," at the expense of those deemed to be outsiders, misfits, sinners, and heretics. Some persons, with a deep need for belonging, may be more inclined to define themselves by who they are not, than who they are. If they are heterosexual, what is easier than to define themselves as not "queer?" Subconsciously, if not consciously, there is a sense of superiority that at least they are not "one of those." Those different than themselves therefore become essential to their self identity and to their sense of belonging. What is the meaning of being "in" unless there are those who are "out?"

All organizations inevitably have issues of exclusion and inclusion. It comes down to the criteria for inclusion. The first great issue the neophyte Church had to deal with was the criteria for inclusion, especially regarding gentiles. Today, for some churches, many of them fundamentalist or evangelical, that criteria effectively includes being, or acting, heterosexual. Homosexuality violates something they regard as inherent to being Christian. Therefore, change, which would bring the outsiders, who they regard as unclean, into the tent, is passionately resisted because that to them would desecrate or defile "their sanctuary." Admission is allowable only on the terms that one repents and converts to the "fundamentals" of this community as defined, usually, by its particular leader. Belonging for them is about conformity not diversity.

Fundamentalism is a closed structure in that belonging requires adherence to a narrow set of principles. The exuberance and joy one sees among them is in part derived from the sense of security found in knowing exactly what the perimeters of grace are and how to stay within them. But there is a dark side. The inner motivation often comes from acceptance of God as the stern and punishing father if one goes outside "His will." There is then just below the surface, a resentment of those who they perceive are outside, and a desire that they not "get away with it." It's the resentment that the older brother (of the prodigal son) feels when his brother returns. The resentment rises in those who live in fear of God's punishment rather than in the bounty of God's grace (though I think most of them would deny that). Anger and resentment surfaces whenever the "liberal" implies that you don't have to believe that God is that ever hovering angry presence.

We had been raised in the Assemblies of God and we always sort of felt that the Assemblies of God preached that God was looking down from heaven with a big huge hammer in his hand and that if you did anything wrong he was going to hit you over the head with his hammer and send you straight to hell.
From "The Eyes of Tammy Faye"

Though there are various ways of defining fundamentalism, historically, theologically, etc., these may take too seriously fundamentalists own casting of themselves as a religious body, or movement (generally a movement, because they see themselves as on a march, or engaged in battle). To understand fundamentalism I believe one must endeavor to look behind its religious expression. Fundamentalists believe that their religion defines who they are. My observation would be that it is the other way around, who they are has defined their religion.

The litmus test of salvation for most fundamentalists has been the "born again" experience, taken from the story of Nicodemus in John 3. Moreover they have a formula for how that must happen, only the formula is comprised of a half dozen prooftexted verses from several New Testament books. The ministry known as The Navigators called this arrangement of verses the "B (baby) rations." These six or eight verses were the beginning ones for their Bible memorization system and formula for infant Christians. If this concoction were the central message of the Gospel would it not be given to us in one passage in its complete form rather than being a bouquet of verses from picking a single verse here and another verse there? And what is the meaning of Jesus statement to Nicodemus, *"You must be born again!"*? Was this story, told in only one of the four gospels, meant to convey the whole meaning of salvation?

That personal experience of being "seized by the power of a great affection," or John Wesley's experience of his heart being "strangely warmed," is to experience the holy. It is beyond rational conception - but NOT in contradiction to it. Those claiming such experience have sometimes used it to try and justify terrible, even monstrous acts of injustice. Moreover, many believe that such an experience implies all that they hold to as "fundamental." But in Matthew 25 Jesus speaks of the separation of the sheep and the goats on the basis of action toward *"the least of these,"* and specifically does so as over against mere religious profession.

The situation of many gays raised in a conservative religious environment is something like that of an abused child. Fear holds them. It is a hook. If they rebel, they fear they will be damned, so many of them conform. The abused child, even as an adult, often defends the abuser repeating what they were told, *"he (God/father) did it because he loves me."* It is what Archie Bunker believed about his father's abuse of him as a child (see chapter 5). Love and abuse become inextricably related in their minds. They love and fear at the same time, daring not to face any contradiction in that.

It is in fact virtually impossible, I think, to stay in some forms of fundamentalism if one does not have, or gives up, that fear of God. Those whose nature it is, or whose experience it is, to believe that God is love - generous, kind, full of grace, welcoming all - will themselves, out of their thanksgiving for God's love tend to be loving and inclusive in the same way. It isn't so much a matter of theology as we pretend. It is a matter of how we experience God's grace.

I am often amazed at the security that some individuals feel to judge others. Where does that come from? If one has a real sense that they are a sinner - not a morbid or self flagellating one - but an honest and realistic sense of their own imperfections, then I think the inclination to judge others is not part of their nature; and whenever there is a situation where it is necessary, they will be guided by compassion and empathy.

I had asked the question, *"In your journey what have you discarded and what have you kept of your initial religious experience?"* John responded: *"I think the thing kept is the original feeling that I had of a family of Christ together - something more than just friends. What you discarded was the fear."*

Recently stores have turned up in many malls selling the art works of Thomas Kincaid. And they sell well - even at $1600. for a single "oil transfer" copy of a 4000 "limited edition." In addition to these "limited editions" there are several other kinds of editions: gallery proofs, artist's proofs, etc., of the same painting. Many who buy these seem to find owning one to be something of a religious experience. That is not without design. This reality is not an unintended one on the part of the artist who in addition to his signature, and a strand of his hair (for DNA authentication) puts John 3:16 on every canvas though that has no specific relationship to the painting.

Kincaid's paintings could be set designs for Disney movies. They are mostly of flower covered cottages on warmly lighted streets, stone stairways, gateways and bridges in garden settings. They have a dreamlike quality.

Though there are rarely people in any of these paintings, there is the implication that within a softly lighted cottage there resides the beatific family. Presumably they are gathered around a hearth, or a bountiful dinner table their heads bowed in grace. Where they most reside though is in the nostalgic feelings and fantasy of many of their viewers.

The clerk in the store of a nearby mall where I went to explore this phenomena dimmed the lights focused on a painting of a small frame church beside a pleasant stream. One could almost hear the sweet sounds of "Amazing Grace" coming from this chapel. He lowered the lights further to show how the lights of the chapel seem almost to shine on their own. (Kincaid bills himself as "the painter of light" - so much for Corot, Carivaggio, Rembrandt or Vermeer). Dimming the lights is part of the standard sales pitch in these galleries. The salesman was merely doing his job but privately (since at the time there was no one else in the store) what he really wanted to talk about was Van Gogh, whose paintings he passionately loves and about whom he had considerable knowledge. I felt for the guy.

Though I am personally put off by the way Christianity is used to market these paintings, it is not my purpose to comment on them as art. People like what they like and they are entitled. Clearly many persons like these paintings very much, paying extraordinary prices for what are almost "unlimited editions." My interest is in understanding this phenomena, which seems to be somewhat a religious one.

I mention these prints because Kincaid's paintings seem to tap into the same feelings that characterize much Christian fundamentalism. Whereas conservatism may be driven by nostalgia, fundamentalism is driven by fantasy. While conservatism may be a locked-on embrace of the past, fundamentalism is an embrace of what never was but that is deeply longed for. It is the longing for that experience of "home" represented in a softly lighted vine covered cottage, or a rose covered garden wall. (Ideas of heaven are constructed of similar images). What many people long for is a sweet calm life by a gently flowing stream, but not life beside the turbulence and commerce of a real river. Perhaps it is longed for because there is much unwanted turbulence in these persons' own lives.

To possess that feeling, they are opposed to whatever they feel brings turbulence or clouds into their picture of how they want life to be. Such a picture must exclude any of the sharp edges or shadows of a real world. That includes the possibility of any romantic and intimate love that is not between a man and woman happily married. The reality of such love between two men, or two women, is not a reality they can allow in their picture of blissful life. Their picture is to them a religious one, and indeed it is very much like what many religious paintings have been. This vision, which has sources that are not Biblical, nonetheless seems to them the one true faith, and they are passionate to exclude from it whatever would change it.

It is difficult to deal with people who are dismissive of reality. There is no solid ground you can get on with them for dialogue. The past, as they reconstruct it, is better than the present, and the ever after, a longed for escape from the now. Their perception seems to be that reality is ugly and that it is better to maintain an optimistic frame of mind by not looking at what to them is unseemly - an abomination. This picture they have is what they think of as holiness; and God, they believe, deals harshly with whatever, as they perceive it, is not holy. I've often heard individuals say that God must commit or allow horrific punishment of the sinner because God, being holy, cannot look upon sin. That statement is the rationalization for many persons' idea that God must bring horrible condemnation on individuals, including gays, who have not, according to their view, properly repented. I marvel that this is received as credible by so many individuals. To say that because God is holy he/she cannot look upon sin is like saying a mother, because she loves her child, cannot look upon dirty diapers. It is a statement that fundamentally denies the incarnation itself, which is God not only looking upon sin but entering flesh, even as a real baby, and as a man walking the roads and streets of sinful humanity. The humanity of Jesus is, therefore, very problematic for them a notion I discuss later in this book.

Reality has within it that which is both dark and light, tragic and beautiful. If we attempt to walk through life with eyes closed, or the lights dimmed, so as not to see ugliness, we would never see light and what light reveals. Jesus' coming is heralded with Isaiah's words, *"The people who walked in darkness have seen a great light and upon them has the light shined."* Light does not come without throwing shadows, nor without revealing what is there, though what is there is sometimes tragic. But only in seeing it is there hope of changing it. What troubles me is that people sometimes see beauty in what doesn't exist, and only ugliness in what does.

I have a dream! Well, maybe it's a premonition, or only a hunch. It is that one day soon some enterprising evangelical leader, perhaps some media evangelist, is going to have a revelation, a change of heart, and is going to give all so-called evangelicals "permission," a green light, to love and accept gays and to fully integrate them without prejudice into the Church.

I am no prophet, and one does not need to be to see some things coming. Within a few years - maybe five, and not likely more than ten - I would not feel surprise if some evangelical, of certified "charisma," were to discover - as some already have - that to be gay and Christian is not an oxymoron after all. A new message will go forth. The message, with chapter and verse, will be something like this: *"Friends, it has come to me that we must declare God's love for all persons and welcome our gay brothers and sisters!"* The unspoken and subconscious text may be, *"We do not want to be on the losing side of history. Now that the mainline denominations - allied with us - have alienated them, let us roll out the welcome mat. Our churches will grow, while theirs continue to shrink."* Conservative politicians will follow when they see the possibility of gaining more votes than they would lose by welcoming gays. In recent elections those running for office seemed already to understand that gays are a constituency they dare not ignore. It's all still the main road, but sometimes if the traffic warrants the main road will be widened.

Sooner than you can say, *"Praise Jesus!"* ministries to welcome gays will spring up in a thousand fundamentalist churches, and this time they won't be talking about "reparative therapy."

This will not be new. This segment of the Church has always seemed to have a windsock atop its steeple to know which way the wind of the Spirit is blowing, and they have always quickly been able to set their sail to it. Theological accommodation - Biblical accommodation - is an art form in which they are well practiced. They will always find the Bible to be quite malleable after all and will quote the scripture in reverse of what they have before, but also, as before, with absolute dogmatism, and their current interpretation will "set up" faster than cement.

If my tone here is cynical it is a reflection of my awareness of the pain they have caused. Nonetheless, if such a change of heart comes, it may indeed be genuine and will be abundantly welcome. If I am cynical, it extends as well to other churches realizing that when the evangelicals no longer obstruct them on this issue, they too will likely change, declaring - not falsely - that that is where their true heart has been all along. The problem is that if their hearts have been in the right place, their feet, up to now, have not. Change may come about largely because the time of many of the old fundamentalist dinosaurs is passing and a younger generation that comes to the fore has experienced the world differently.

I'd like to know if some conservatives, having fought for many years to prevent certain changes in the life of the Church, and society, would now, if they could, go back and have things the way they were. Would they now want things to be the way they aggressively fought to keep them? Not likely!

Of those not categorized as "mainline" - some fundamentalists and some evangelicals - when they need to find a Biblical rationale to change they will no doubt, as they have in the past over other issues, be remarkably resourceful. They will also seem to be largely unaware and unrepentant of the incredible harm they have done. It has happened before with racial integration and the ordination of women.

Much of the institutional Church is rapidly losing its credibility over her inability to bring herself to a truly open and heartfelt embrace of gay, lesbian, bisexual, and transgender persons. The realities of a post-Christian era loom. Whatever she does now, the moment - the historical moment - to lead will already have been missed. Whatever happens now can only look like the Church was dragged into it, ironically, by the moral evolution of the popular culture. The institutional Church will finally only have opened her heart, her doors, and her structures because she has been shamed into it, or because some have recognized that it has become more expedient to Church growth and institutional survival to be inclusive than exclusive.

Why do I not credit people with having acted out of honest moral conviction? The problem I believe has been an unwillingness by some of those who are supposed to provide a moral compass to address in themselves the bias that distorts their own Biblical and theological understanding.

When I was ordained in 1965, in Arlington, Virginia (suburban Washington D.C., nonetheless it was the South), many Presbyterians were fighting hard to keep their churches, neighborhoods and schools, racially segregated. They lost that battle. Do they now regret that such segregation, at least overtly, is gone? It wouldn't seem so. Today, whatever interracial experience they can claim, especially if they can find some way to take credit for it, they are proud of. Their segregationist attitudes seem now to be conveniently forgotten.

Today almost all persons in the Church would be loathe to be thought of as racist, or sexist, just as they are loathe to be thought of as homophobic. Conservative institutions not only welcome Blacks but are apt to show them off to illustrate that they are not racist. Even in this showcasing, African-Americans are put at the service of others. Bob Jones University (which for decades billed itself as "the world's most unusual University" - and lived up to it) would like to enhance itself politically by leaving behind some of its racist past.

Most conservatives no longer openly discriminate against women in the clergy, or other offices of the Church. Who would call them sexist now? But they were - to the teeth! They resisted, and obstructed, in every way they could, the integration of African-Americans, and women. They lost, and now they cannot even seem to remember that they were ever there. Have they acknowledged what they did? Have they repented of any of it? There is little evidence that they have.

Though many conservatives fought hard to keep women out of the clergy - firing Bible verses from their trenches - they lost. Would they go back, if they could, to an all male clergy? Not likely, given that seminaries, theirs included, now train for ordination hundreds of women as ministers of Word and Sacrament. In Presbyterian churches women predominate on many of their Boards of Elders, and Boards of Deacons. Like their racial attitudes, some of their sexist attitudes are now conveniently forgotten. Have they changed? Today many conservatives are doing everything they can to keep gays and lesbians disempowered in the Church.

They have now fought for over twenty five years against the ordination of self-affirming gay or lesbian Christians. They provided the "Biblical" rational for those who did the bashing during the AIDS epidemic, the rise in hate crimes against lesbians and gays, and the alarming incidence of adolescent suicide related to sexual orientation. They did not throw the stones, but those who did laid their cloaks at their feet, so to speak, so that they, like Saul, were in effect "consenting" to this stoning (Acts 7:54-8:1). They managed to lend encouragement, even if unwittingly, to these crimes.

Again, as in the past, they now act with moral certainty that there can be no way but their way. When they have sensed that they are on the wrong side of history, and have "rediscovered" the Gospel, will there be shame and repentance for all the struggle and injury they have caused? Most likely what there will be, as there has been, is - amnesia.

Fundamentalism is cultic in nature in that it is a religious movement centered on charismatic personalities. This gives it an enormous freedom of movement as compared to mainline denominations which in their more democratic structures must build consensus for change. Fundamentalism is often intractable in its capacity for stunning shifts, for hairpin turns. Her positions can change in a fortnight, by the word of permission from a current media evangelist or guru, to serve something which is at the core of fundamentalism. What is at the core?

Their core issue it seems is an idolatrous devotion to a certain concept of family. This family is basically hierarchical, and devoutly heterosexual. This accounts for her attitudes about abortion, public education, women's issues, welfare, & creationism. All are traceable to this patriarchal, hierarchical family.

Fundamentalism is the cult of the American family. It uses Christianity and the Bible to try and authenticate itself, but, in fact its values and its ethos actually have little real connection to the heart or essence of either of these. It does make an ample use of the Old Testament culture of patriarchy, and totally misses Jesus condemnation of that. It is a religion of fear, fear that what they regard as family is being undermined by "alternative" families, families that have a different configuration than what to them is essential. In their view, fatherhood, motherhood, and marriage are undermined. It is fear that their children who may not have this same set of feelings, because it relates to a world they never knew, will get away from them, live in relationships they do not approve, and have values different than their own.

During his adolescence David's mother feared that he might be veering from the faith...

Our church had dedication where you could take your child up and dedicate its life to Christ. I remember when I was a teenager and very rebellious, my mother would in her most furious voice say to me, "It doesn't matter what you do, we dedicated your life to Christ." I said, "Well, it wasn't yours to give."

Control therefore is everything. It is not surprising that one verse virtually every one of them knows is, "*spare the rod and spoil the child.*" A "rod," by the way, is not a mere open hand on the buttocks intended more to direct a child's attention than to inflict pain. A rod is meant to inflict great pain and is apt to also cause injury. When I was a kid the razor strap, paddle, or willow whip, were regarded by many as appropriate instruments of discipline. Daddies were expected to be the enforcers. *"Just you wait till your dad gets home!"* They trust no external institution including public schools. They respond to politicians who promise smaller government, which they interpret as less government control and more personal hands on control for them. And they have a thirst for theocracy.

Ironically, though they want no government interference in regard to regulating business, guns, the environment, and "their" public schools; they are adamant in wanting the government and the courts to intrude into and to regulate the most personal and intimate aspects of the lives of others; a woman's right to choose, gays in the military, the arts, free speech, sexual relations, etc., whatever they deem subversive to their "family values."

With the fundamentalist's emphasis on family it is unfortunate that many of them seem so unaware or uncaring of the great harm that they do to families by their own teaching and practice of discrimination and intolerance. Homosexuals belong to families. They have parents, siblings, and grandparents, aunts and uncles; and among gays the stories are nearly endless of the painful, disruptive effect religion has had on their families. Today ythcgmost extended families, if not immediate families, have within them an "out" gay or lesbian member. Dobson's, "Focus on the Family," focuses only on those families of which they approve.

There is also the failure and unwillingness of many to acknowledge what they characterize as "alternative families" as being as real and as significant as their own. There is implicit condescension even in the term alternative family. These families have many configurations (some of which have nothing to do with gays) but gay couples are family, and today many of them are families with children.

Heterosexuals often object to gay adoption and would sometimes seem almost to prefer that children have no family than to have gay parents. Gay couples who want children, and that is many, are in most instances a wonderful source of adoptive parents. And it would certainly help if we honored their relationships as covenantal as we do heterosexual couples. In virtually any instance I have seen they are extraordinary parents, first because they are highly motivated to be parents, and secondly because they usually have very keen sensitivity to the emotional life of children growing out of their own experiences of being gay in this society.

Do the fundamentalists' ideas about family arise from who God is, or is God conceived to be what they derive from their own particular family structure? They are obsessed with a vision of the beatific family. Where in scripture does that family exist? It doesn't.

Many self-certifying "born-againers" have now forged themselves as a political constituency in America, usually as part of the conservative wing of the Republican Party. There is a veritable assumption by them that to be born-again means to be a political conservative, and especially to embrace a certain political dogma that includes being anti-abortion, for the death penalty, against gun control, in favor of prayer in public schools, and to oppose what they call "the gay agenda." To disagree with any of their "agenda" would be for many fundamentalists to cast doubt on whether that individual is truly "born again." They often use the term "Christians" as applying only to themselves, and "the Word of God," as being only their interpretation of it. Having become a toted political constituency, being "born again" now seems to imply not only a set of religious convictions but a set of political convictions as well. Scripture has been employed by many fundamentalists not so much for what it tells us about God, truth, and wisdom; as for how it can be used to sanction prevailing culture and existing prejudice. More and more it is distorted to serve their political agenda.

Apart from their stance against abortion, fundamentalists and conservatives have not shown themselves to be particularly sensitive on issues related to the sanctity of life. Many of them are strong supporters of the death penalty (a strange way to try and make the point that life is sacred); most are reluctant to worry about the effects of uncontrolled gun ownership, or God's creatures killed for sport, or lost through environmental damage. Albert Sweitzer's "reverence for life" is light years from their thinking.

For fundamentalists, the '60's represents the beginning of moral decline in America. The nostalgia and the idolatry toward a certain model of family that characterizes fundamentalism is based on the illusion of a sweet moral society before the '60s. The cinnamony smell of apple pie hovers over it. I, however, have lived long enough to remember a more than detectable stench. It is not a Norman Rockwell world fundamentalists long for (Rockwell hung close to the real world); it is a Thomas Kincaid fantasy of the world.

They look around and can see nothing but the loss of innocence. The movie "Pleasantville" did an interesting take on this. An adolescent boy finds himself hooked on a television soap called "Pleasantville" (think Ozzie and Harriet). When the remote control of his TV goes out, a "strange" TV repairman appears unsolicited; and when the young man clicks the "repaired" remote, he finds himself drawn into the TV and lands in Pleasantville. The town and the townsfolk, like the TV show, are in black and white. The drama which unfolds is one in which these black and white persons, as real things happen to them, become real themselves, and (if you will pardon the inadvertent pun) become persons of color. The point of course is obvious, those who see all things as black and white do not see the real world, or real people. And though reality is far more complex, and often painful, it is also infinitely more wonderful.

Over the last several years I've reflected many times on the extraordinary rage by some against Bill - and Hillary - Clinton. Where, I have wondered with many others, does this rage (and there seems no other word for it) come from? Perhaps it is that he was the first baby-boomer president, the first to have come of age in the 1960's, after what many naively and falsely recall as the age of innocence.

> *"Why do you hate Clinton so much?"*
>   an interviewer asked a Chicago conservative during
>   the impeachment hearings
> *"His policies have not been particularly radical."*
> *"I'll tell you why I hate Clinton..."*
>   the activist responded,
> *"I hate him because he's a womanizing, Elvis-loving, noninhaling, truth-shading, war-protesting, draft-dodging, abortion-protecting, gay-promoting, gun-hating baby boomer. That's why! It's the values, stupid."*
>   William Schneider L. A. Times, Dec. 31, 2000

It's interesting that he mentions "Elvis-loving" because Elvis - a southern boy who loved his mother, and sang hymns - fits in quite well now with fundamentalist values even though at one time they fostered hysteria over his moving pelvis; another example of conservative accommodation.

Civil Rights (which they saw as the homogenization of the culture), Viet Nam war resistance, Rock and Roll, Woodstock, and Stonewall, represented for them this decline. Conveniently forgotten is what happened to Jews, Blacks, Asians, and homosexuals in their vision of America before the 60's. They also seem not to remember McCarthyism. Amnesia again. I am old enough to remember these well, and in specific detail, and I will not forget them, because to forget is to not be alert that they may too easily come again.

There was much that was not good about the sixties - particularly drugs; but far from being a time when morality was discarded, it was a time when a younger generation saw themselves as earnestly engaged in a moral revolution, the dawning of the Age of Aquarius.

Responding to a question I asked about what they would want to say to others, Gerald identified with that revolution.

...maybe I'm back in the 60's, but what comes to mind is...I would tell people, "Try to embrace the other." I still have a vision of one world, one universe, whatever you want to call it. I believe in opening oneself up to really try to understand everything and every person who is not me. I think it is that which is really at the heart of the Gospel as well. It has led me to a more true and satisfying spirituality.

Chapter 3

The Fixers

> *"...after about six months of therapy....I was feeling the same way I had, and I didn't see any real hope for change. And at that point I said, "What shall I do, how can I change?" And he suggested aversion therapy, which is basically you look at erotic pictures of men if you're homosexual, and then they charge your brain with enough electricity to drop a cow. Over a period of time, you learn that looking at pictures of naked men is a painful experience and therefore you eliminate that from your life....I asked the psychiatrist., "Now just to be sure we're on the same track here, if I go through this I'll end up being heterosexual?' "No," he said, "but you won't be homosexual.'"*
>
> Paul
> (from Lazarus video, "Scared to Death")

For some religious persons reality doesn't matter that much if you are trying to resolve a theological problem because since God can do anything no problem really exists. God, they believe, does not want anyone to be homosexual (meaning they do not want anyone to be homosexual), therefore God will change them, and they will assist God in doing that. They will be the fixers. If they can't fix what they regard as "sexual brokenness," and God doesn't fix them to actually be heterosexual, they believe they can help the really committed ones to not be homosexual.

There has been some hedging of late on the initial claims of sexual "reorientation." There is more acknowledgement today, even among those in the so called "ex-gay ministries," that sexual orientation is not chosen, and even some acknowledgment that it cannot in some persons be changed. Much of that change of attitude is due to their own poor track record, and to the position now of almost all the therapeutic disciplines, The American Psychiatric Association, The American Psychological Association, the American Medical Association, etc., that sexual orientation cannot be changed and that those who practice "reparative therapy" may in fact be doing harm. What is left is the hope and conviction that at least some highly motivated persons encumbered with this "moral defect" (those with sufficient shame and guilt) can live lives of sexual abstinence.

Gay persons who are made to feel that they are not acceptable to God as they are and cannot change, often come to the point of wondering if God is just jerking them around. Having a nature they did not choose and cannot change they feel, or are told, that God condemns them for its expression, or demands an unnatural and inhumane abstinence. If this is what a God of love does, then the meaning of love itself is distorted.

There are many small theaters in West Hollywood and Hollywood, and many of their productions have gay themes. A few years ago one of these productions, "Southern Baptist Sissies," was something of a phenomena, having consistently full houses and a number of extensions of its original run. It was written by Del Shore (writer and director of the film, "Sordid Lives"), who clearly knows of what he writes.

The play is the story of four boys growing up, and growing up gay, in a Southern Baptist church in Texas. In the play, one of them, having grown into his adulthood and experienced some of the struggle endemic to his orientation, asks the question, *"Is God just f---ing with us?"* Though crudely put, this manner of asking gives it some of the emotional heft it deserves. Though a legitimate, and for many, an existential theological question, most of the Church does not answer it because she does not ask it.

A true answer relies on a right question rightly asked. The Church often has no valid answer because she rejects all the real questions. If God is believed to require what one did not choose and cannot change, and God does not choose to change them, then this would surely seem to be a God capricious and cruel in nature, demanding of his/her presumably beloved creature that which that creature has no power to be or to give.

Many persons seem untroubled by the theological contradiction in claiming that God is love and yet God's behavior is cruel. The reality is that God is often used as cover by those whose own attitudes are cruel. The depth of cruelty is evidenced in some fundamentalists' reaction to the AIDS epidemic. While they - those infected and those who loved them - coped with a holocaust, others in the name of Christ declared this to be God's punishment. Canadian evangelist, Ken Campbell, a longtime opponent of gay rights, a few years ago in a demonstration at the Ontario Superior Court against the issuing of marriage licenses to gay couples, referred to Toronto's Gay Pride Parade as the "*AIDS parade*."

I was well acquainted with a woman, now deceased, whose gay son died of AIDS. At his funeral service in the Presbyterian Church to which the family belonged the minister used the occasion to preach on the sin of homosexuality and the punishment that God inflicts on those who practice it. The mother, in enormous grief, was so outraged that she became from that time forward until her own death, a tireless advocate for gay and lesbian persons.

Is God just jerking gays around? Toying with them? Is this something like the story of Job and God is testing, or allowing the testing, of gays because of some wager God has made with the devil? If God wills a thing, and another wills the same thing, willing what he or she has been told is God's will, then what is the problem? Did Jesus not say, *"ask and you shall receive;"* and *"if one asks for bread will he be given a stone?"* Why is the person not then what others think God wills them to be? Is God unable? Or is God unwilling to affect that which God presumably requires? Either of those possibilities is clearly irrational though many Christians insist that is the way God is. Does that not say, *"If God is God He is not good, if good He is not God?"*

What I felt - was betrayed. I'd been told I'd be cured. And if I wasn't cured that meant my faith was weak - that somehow I hadn't given it all over to God, I hadn't completely surrendered. So basically, if I wasn't cured, it was my fault. It is so awful. Not only was I gay - which God didn't like - but apparently I didn't have enough faith to change it. Anyway, I just kept praying and praying and asking God to change me until I finally gave up.... The funny thing is that down deep I never really thought there was anything wrong with me. If no one had told me to hate being gay, I don't think it would have occurred to me. I wish I'd known to listen to that inner voice, but I was just a kid.

David

I don't feel at all that God has done this to us. I think that is something that over time human beings have done to each other and have projected that on God...

Neal

When I think of the AIDS crisis that's been so devastating, I don't think it's from God..., but it certainly is a terrible thing that has affected our community to a great extent. And being in The Gay Mens' Chorus we've had over

a hundred persons in the chorus who have died. I have friends that have died of AIDS - close friends.
                              Allen

The testimony even of those who defend the so-called "ex-gay ministries" is that maybe God doesn't change everyone who wills it, or change them completely, or immediately. Why not?

Fundamentalists are not ones who believe that Jesus healed only some who came to him asking for healing. Nor do they believe that Jesus healed lepers, the lame, the blind, the deaf - incrementally? It does not speak well of God to suggest that among the many praying to be changed God picks and chooses a few and to be told that even such change will be exceedingly gradual and perhaps never complete. What is the model for that in scripture? Did Jesus ever say, *"not you, but him"*...and *"not now, but later"*...or *"gradually, very gradually, if you're good."*?

Is it not all a desperate effort not to acknowledge that sexual orientation is not chosen and cannot be changed? Where do we look in the Gospels? Jesus is the model of what God is and what God wills and what God has the power to perform, so we look to the gospels, but where does Jesus, when one comes begging for healing, put them off or make them grovel for years to obtain that mercy? What kind of a gospel would that be? It certainly would be a gospel without good news. Where does Jesus require self denigration, years of agony and travail to "maybe" - but not likely - obtain what presumably both God and the individual have willed all along? Is God a liar, a procrastinator, a hypocrite, a manipulator, a sadist?

What we judge about others becomes judgments we make about God. We should consider what we are saying in these instances. We are not talking, you understand, about fighting against one's nature, we all sometimes must do that, but asking *"what stands in the way, if both God and the homosexual agree, of that nature being changed?"* Yes, to gain the acceptance, if not approval of others, individuals might behave contrary to their nature. But that is in fact to act in an "unnatural" way - for some supposed divine good.

I went into the military. I was about to be drafted into the army because I had quit college. Well, I joined the Air Force instead...In the military I was involved in different chapel programs. My background at that time was very fundamentalist, Pentecostal. I knew by then I was gay. I really fought against acting on it all through the military, but then when I got out I was tired of fighting... I went to this conference in Anaheim (Melodyland)....Two guys spoke and said they were ex-gays....I went to their class and the classroom was so full of people that I had to sit out in the doorway...., There were gay and lesbian people there....and they (the ex-gays) wanted to help them.... So I went to counseling there, from the Valley to Orange County, for nearly a year for this "therapy." They were pretty honest that they couldn't change a person's orientation, but they felt they could help you to not be with gay friends or live the gay "lifestyle." But it didn't work....here were a whole lot of gay people....

I really had not acted on being gay. I still had a tremendous amount of guilt.... There's a park near my house and a restroom and five guys were hanging out there when I came home from work, so I figured something was going on....I went there and I met this guy and he was in a voice class of mine at college, and (he) said, "Have you been to The Lodge?" "What's that?" He said it was a gay bar. I had a lot of fear and I'd never been to a gay bar, and he said, "Let's go to The Lodge." So reluctantly I went with him, and though I was very afraid... when I got in there people were very nice. And I went every night - something new to do. At least in my experience of going through that whole exit thing I learned a lot about the gay community....though I tried hard to change.

I went through all that therapy stuff in Orange County - nothing worked, and so I just came to the realization that I'm gay and to deal with it. And I knew that's what I had to do because nothing would change my sexual orientation.

           Allen

Underlying the issue of sexual orientation for many is the fear that what is really at stake is the meaning of male and female. Everyone has a sexual orientation, but it is an orientation, and beneath this in all persons, as part of their biological makeup, is the plain sexual force, drive, or hunger (whatever one chooses to call it) which is altogether unbiased as to object. It is the orientation that directs our sexuality toward one person rather than another, toward one gender more than another. Sexual orientation is more complex than we generally care to admit. The world does not divide neatly into straight and gay, nor into straight, gay, and bisexual; and not always does it divide neatly into male and female, especially those characteristics we may be inclined to associate with gender.

  The closet, so much a part of the life of gay persons, has also been a cage. The very situation of their being in such a cage seems to imply guilt. Gays have not only been coming out of the closet, they have also been struggling to get out of that defendant's cage. Thoughtful, self-affirming gays reject the too common assumption that they should offer a defense of themselves regardless of how sensitive, compassionate, or broad-minded some who judge them may consider themselves to be. They rightly maintain they have no more need to defend or explain themselves than do heterosexual persons. Many of them not only do not regard their sexual orientation as a fault, defect, weakness, or sin; they consider it a gift. The question as to why they are homosexual has no more relevance than the question as to why someone is heterosexual.

Though many gays at one time tried desperately to change their orientation, simply to make their lives more bearable in the midst of a very homophobic society, many have now matured to a point of healthy self-acceptance. If a way were known to change from being homosexual to heterosexual, most of them would feel no moral obligation to take it, and would not choose, if they could, to change. A medical doctor I know, who is gay, exclaimed to me with obvious joy that he was delighted to be a gay man. He said it as if, "How did I get so lucky?" He was one who happened also to come out of a Pentecostal background.

The incessant debate over whether sexual orientation is nature or nurture is appropriately of genuine scientific interest and investigation, but from a moral standpoint it is irrelevant. We are what we are.

The nature/nurture question is of great significance to conservatives because they hope to make from it an argument that an orientation is the product of nurture and therefore persons can be "reoriented." This is the rationale for so-called reparative therapy (which is neither reparative nor therapy). Those who choose to believe that others' sexual orientation can be changed usually use some outdated theory or pop psychology to try to make their case. Evidence that these theories are false simply do not interest them where it conflicts with their presumptions.

The only people who believe that change is possible are those people who believe that change should be possible, and that is very suspicious. Anybody who doesn't have a vested interest in change just looks at the evidence and is honest, and says, "that isn't happening."
Ralph Blair, "Christian" psychologist

Many persons who have a "gut feeling" that homosexuality is wrong will see what they want to see, hear what they want to hear, and embrace whatever arguments seem to support that feeling. For them, that feeling seems rooted in an idea of holiness and cleanliness found in the Bible. But the "gut feeling" they have, which seems to them infallible, is not usually one taken from scripture but one with which they go to scripture seeking affirmation. There are many who are fond of saying "hate the sin, love the sinner." What they believe is that it is love to want gays to become what they approve. That is not love!

Hearing and reading the testimonies of individuals who feel that a homosexual who enters into any same sex relationship is committing sin, I feel compassion for many of these persons who, according to their own stories have been through tragic and sometimes brutal experiences. It is not too difficult to understand their deep need for self-affirmation which they believe can only come from identifying themselves as not gay. They believe that because much of the Church incessantly tells them that. In their testimonies they almost invariably refer to the fact that though they believe their sexual orientation has been, or is being changed, they still "struggle" with old temptations. Here are quotes from some of these testimonies:

"I am even thankful that I still experience some degree of same-sex erotic desires, because they remind me that I am totally dependent on Christ."

"...I then felt as if God asked me one of the hardest questions I've ever had to answer: 'Are you willing to deal

with these temptations for the rest of your life?'...I rarely experience homosexual thoughts (now) and genuinely desire to be a wife and mother."

"I'm very much in the process of restoration, a process that God started. I know God has promised to finish the work He's begun in me. That gives me hope..."

"This process of transformation was not an easy one, but as I let people in my Presbyterian church know about involvement in this ministry, I receive prayer, acceptance and encouragement not to give up...that acceptance encouraged me to continue, even when it got tough."

"God is helping me to address the hurts, lies and wounds that have led to my sense of inadequacy as a man. As a result, I no longer identify myself as a homosexual, and my same-sex attractions have diminished. I have accepted that I am still in process, that all things don't change over night."

"This process has been challenging and agonizing, with progress and setbacks, triumph and pain. At times I have made mistakes and poor choices. ...Change is a continuing process for me, but without it my growth would have leveled off and stagnation would have set in."

"I am still tempted sometimes to return to the homosexual lifestyle. My hope is in the Lord. I sometimes fall. My hope is in the Lord. I was depressed, beaten and hopeless, but my hope is in the Lord. I was dead and filthy in sin, but the Lord washed me and redeemed me and my life is in His hands."

"The process of coming out of homosexuality has not been easy. However, God's love and faithfulness have sustained me. I have great compassion for those who are still struggling with their sexuality."

"I can honestly admit to you that my same-sex feelings have greatly diminished. They no longer have to control me or define me as a person. I've experienced freedom and now recognize my choices. There hasn't been a 'curing of my homosexuality,' so to speak, but an ongoing healing of my emotional wounds."

Common to these particular testimonies is in what is stated in this last quotation, "...an ongoing healing of my emotional wounds." Despite the fact that virtually all of the therapeutic disciplines and organizations now reject the idea that a homosexual orientation is a pathology, this and other organizations still choose to define it as the result of some form of emotional trauma. The healing of "sexual brokenness" is their most common definition of their "ministry."

What I consistently do not hear, both in these written testimonies, and in conversations I have had with others from these "change" ministries, is a plain declaration that the person was decidedly homosexual and now is decidedly heterosexual. There is almost always some hedging on this, some qualifying statement. The words "process" and "struggle" come up repeatedly. While I commend the honesty of that, it begs the theological question. If they believe God hates their homosexuality and they accept that it is sin and repent and pray to be what they believe God requires of them, then why are they not totally changed? Though there is no doubt some measure of bisexuality in almost all persons, the meaning of heterosexual and homosexual is not completely ambiguous.

Though I have respect and compassion for many engaged in trying to change their sexual orientation, I don't believe that persons with a true heterosexual orientation "struggle" continually against homosexual temptation. I am concerned that these individuals, many of whom are still young, are going to find their attraction is still to those of the same gender. If, seeking love, they "fall" from their resolve not to be gay, they are likely for a time to become self-hating. That is not an uncommon journey. I know a number of individuals who have been in various "change" ministries, and were deeply earnest in their intention. It not only did not change their orientation, it sometimes led them for a while down a self-destructive path. I am also concerned that many of those attempting not to be who they are will choose marriage as cover for their homosexual feelings. This will exploit another person.

Most of these individuals are earnestly trying to cope with the negative messages that have been sent to them, especially by the Church. They are also being used by the Church irresponsibly as illustrations that homosexuality is sin and that sexual orientation can be changed.

Chapter 4

Faith of Our Fathers - Living Still

"...coming from a fundamentalist perspective, God the father ruled in the (same) sense that father controlled the family that I grew up in. There was more a sense of sternness than any kind of love. The fear element was very large. I had difficulty reconciling my feelings about it because feelings weren't a part of that masculinity. Things were rigid, pretty clear, they were right or wrong. My biological father and my heavenly father formed a total image of God in my early years."

Gerald

There is an episode of "All In the Family" that I remember particularly well. After years of America watching that extraordinary sitcom, in this episode we were given a deep insight into why Archie was, well - Archie. It was probably in its last season when Archie has the tavern. In this episode Michael (Meathead) is helping his father-in-law close up the tavern for the night. They carry some cases into the back storeroom, and Archie accidentally leaves the key in the lock on the outside of the door. The door closes and they are locked in. There is no phone, no one can hear them and they have no choice but to stay there until morning when the bartender comes to open up. They get into some of their usual sparring.

Archie: *"You're only locked in here with me. Look who I'm locked in here with.?"*

Michael complains that Archie always calls him "Meathead," and Archie tells about when he was a kid and the name they called him. His family was very poor and he lost one of his shoes. However he had a boot from a pair, one of which he had also lost, so his mother had him wear the shoe, with the boot on the other foot. After that the kids at school started calling him "shoebootie." Locked in the storeroom time passes, they drink and get slightly drunk. Archie begins to talk about his childhood and tells about getting beat up by a black kid who he had called "nigger." Archie doesn't see anything wrong with that because that is what his father called them.

Meathead: *"Did you ever think your old man might possibly have been wrong."*

Archie: (a nerve has been struck) *My old man? Don't be stupid. Let me tell you something about him, he was never wrong about nothin."*

Meathead: *"Yes he was Arch. You're father was wrong. Let me tell you something. My father used to call people the same things as your old man, but I always knew he was wrong. So was your old man."*

Archie: *"No, he wasn't!"*

Meathead: *"Yes, he was!"*

Archie: *"He wasn't!"*

Meathead: *"Your father was wrong!!!"*

Archie: *"Don't tell me my father was wrong. Let me tell you something. God don't make wrong your father; the breadwinner of the house there, a man who goes out and busts his butt to keep a roof over your head and clothes on your back. You call your father wrong? Hey, this is your father...your father! He comes home bringing you candy. Your father's the first guy to throw a baseball to you, and take you for walks in the park holding you by the hand. My father, he held me by the hand.* (Archie holds up his own hand.) *My father had a hand on him - now I tell you. He busted that hand once, and he busted it on me...to teach me good. My father shoved me in the closet for seven hours to teach me to do good...because he loved me...he loved me."*

(Meathead is listening intently, clearly seeing Archie as he has never seen him.)

Archie: *"Oh, don't be looking at me. Let me tell you, you're suppose to love your father because your father loves you; and how can any man who loves you tell you anything that's wrong."* (Archie, tired, expended, and slightly drunk lies down to sleep). *"Oh, what's the use of talking."*

Meathead covers him tenderly with an old awning they have found in the storeroom.

Meathead: (softly) *"Goodnight, shoebootie."*

Archie Bunker is the archetype of many American males in the twentieth century. Maybe what we always sensed in him was the child bucking up to be a man in his father's eyes. Distorted as it is, there is a fierce morality in Archie. The tremendous success of "All in the Family" is largely because of how accurately Norman Lear touched upon this archetype and tapped into something in our collective unconscious, and with an actor who could perfectly convey him.

Honor thy father and mother - especially "thy father," - is the FIRST commandment for many men. It lies near the core of their religion, though they may not know it. Ancestor - patriarchal - worship is not far from the Judeo-Christian religion, nor far from many other religions. Our gods are tribal gods, and our fathers are the heads of our tribes. For many it is how they know who they are, and how they know what they are to do.

Transpose Archie's feelings into the concept of God as father and one has an idea of the origin of some persons' religion. God the Father for many is understood as being like their own father, even in instances where their own father was abusive. So their religious feelings are often ambivalent and conflicted as are the feelings that some men have regarding their own fathers. These conflicted feelings may be especially real for gay men who have grown up in a fundamentalist religious environment. What is often missing for them is any sense of God as nurturer. It is missing because that is perceived as a feminine role. God, it seems to many cannot be feminine because the feminine, they perceive, is not the head but the helpmate. Under patriarchy in scripture woman is a derivative of man, as in the creation of Eve taken from Adam's rib. Historically the patriarchal nature of Roman Catholicism is relieved by the incorporation of Mary as a divine intercessor.

Many persons' idea of God as father is drawn from their own experience of father; fathers that are stern lawgivers and enforcers; fathers that are rigid and punishing; fathers who can only show their love as reward for obedience; fathers not prone to the softness and sympathies of women. And they are those kinds of fathers because that's how their fathers were before them.

The cultural expectation is that a boy will take his gender identification from his father, and a girl from her mother. Sometimes that doesn't happen. There are no simple and no universal reasons for that. It happens. Sometimes it happens differently even for identical twins. Some fathers may feel they have failed to produce a masculine son, or that it is a silent rebellion of the child against his father. Usually it is neither. But it may cause some emotional estrangement between the father and the son, which the son is often in his own life trying to overcome.

Since many gay men have often sought in their lover a substitute for their punishing or emotionally inaccessible father, a lover who heals the wounds inflicted by the father, they can perhaps understand God better under this different paradigm of lover rather than father. (Saying this I would, however, caution that the emotionally distant father is by no means a universal experience of gay men, and is a too facile explanation of a homosexual orientation in men.)

Sometimes gay men seek to replicate the abusive father associating abuse with love. One wonders if Martin Luther's austerity and self-flagellation as an Augustinian monk had something to do with his own troubled relationship with his father, and also with the father figures of his ecclesiastical superiors, including the Pope (papa). Luther's conversion is a breaking free from the coercive relationship he had with his father. Similarly, St. Francis' rebellion against his father, repudiating the wealth and privilege into which he had been born, seems to have been catalyst for his spiritual awakening and his chosen poverty and simple life

What is needed is an image of God, neither male nor female, who loves us unconditionally, not necessarily according to a parent/child model (though I'd not exclude that altogether), but loves us as a friend. We journey with this friend, the friend journeys with us. There are "trials and tribulations" but the friend does not leave us. It is a relationship that redeems us, day by day. Today is the day of our salvation, as yesterday was and tomorrow will be. *"WHAT A FRIEND WE HAVE IN JESUS,"* is true. There is language in some old gospel hymns that fits very well with the experience of many gay men, just as it fits with the experience of African-Americans. It is a kind of grassroots theology that arises from the heart of oppressed persons.

From a dream sequence in Christopher Fry's verse drama, "A Sleep of Prisoners," is this dialogue as they sleep...
> Peter (in the dream he is Isaac): *"Where is the creator that has to die? There's nothing here of any life worth taking...a flinching snail, a few unhopeful harebells."*
> David (in the dream he is Abraham): *"What else?"*
> Peter (as Isaac) *"You, father, and me...Are you going to kill me? No! Father! I've come only a short way into life and I can see great distance waiting...surely there's no need for us to be the prisoners of the dark. Smile, father. Let me go."*
> David (as Abraham): *"...the cords bind you against my will but you're bound for a better world. And I must lay you down to sleep for a better waking. Come now."*

Of the many horrific stories cheerfully told by a variety of Sunday School teachers, the one that was most terrifying to my young mind was the story of Abraham's intended sacrifice of Isaac. I can only assume that my Sunday School teacher, who otherwise seemed like a nice lady, was so glazed over with piety that she had no real comprehension that the story she was telling to children was a horror story. To her it spoke only of the goodness of God, since God intervened and prevented the old man from actually burying the knife into his own son whom he had strapped and laid on his makeshift altar. Actually she may have just been following the prescribed Sunday School curriculum.

I'm maybe age 8 or 9 when I first hear this story. I'm thinking, *"My God, you believe that is a good God who sets up this old man to actually intend to make a ritual slaughter of his son as a test of his loyalty?"* For those who find something commendable in Abraham's intent to sacrifice his son, what is their opinion of Andrea Yate's drowning of her five children as an act of holiness? Or the former body guard of Osama Bin Laden, interviewed on television, who spoke of his hope that his nine year old son would in a few years strap a bomb to his body and blow himself up for the sake of Allah. Even if in the end the old man offers a ram instead, how is the son ever supposed to recover from what his father intended to do? Talk about childhood trauma. Try to get over one like that.

One interpretation I heard from a Jewish source is that the story merely describes a ritualistic rather than a real intended sacrifice and that, in fact, Isaac was not a child but a grown man. Still it presents the ram as a substitution for a real human sacrifice, and thereby depicts God as requiring blood sacrifice.

"God was testing Abraham," the teacher explained. Testing? No, a spelling bee is a test. A math quiz is a test. For God to instruct you to murder your own son to demonstrate faithfulness, it is not simply a test, it is an act of psychological terror.

Testing, I learned, was the rationale for a lot of what God did. Eve got tested, and Adam, and Noah, and Jonah, and Moses, and Hosea, and most especially Job got tested with his children dying, being bankrupted, and breaking out in boils. When Job asks some pretty legitimate questions as to why this testing, the only answer he gets is in the whirlwind - that answer being that God being God is not answerable to Job for his suffering.

The thing about God's testing is that ultimately everybody fails, and there is no grading on the curve. This is called "universal depravity." Snuggle up to this God if you can. Even at ten or twelve I was becoming pretty cynical and not inclined to regard this tester as a "God of love." Every bad thing that happens to an individual can be attributed to God. Either the bad thing is a trial or a test (as with Job), or it is God's discipline or punishment for a bad deed done. In Germany and Austria, as we were soon to learn, millions of Jews were being exterminated by every available means. Was this a test, or was it a punishment? During the AIDS epidemic that same question became existential again for many gay men. Was this a test? Or as many in the religious community brutally suggested, a punishment?

Old Abraham was willing to sacrifice - murder - his own son because he believed that was what God wanted him to do, and what God wants God gets. Why? Because who can argue with God? Abraham didn't ask if God was good, he simply knew God was bigger. God had to help Abraham know that he was not only bigger but that he was good.

Should it matter to us that God is good rather than just all powerful? Is what God wants of us simple obedience, no questions asked, to arbitrary laws for laws sake, having no need in our theology to be related to any human concept of logic, justice, or mercy? Does it really not matter if God condemns what persons did not choose and cannot change and yet is fundamental to their humanity?

In time, my own conviction, in the context of what had become my own faith experience, was that one makes allowances. They, of course, are not allowances made for God. Who can make allowances for God? That's irrational. But allowances can be made for the tellers of the stories. I could accept that this is the story of the exodus of a wandering Aramaean (Deuteronomy 26:5) out of his native culture - and there is a lot of residue of that in Abraham. In this exodus he stumbles toward a new, and, all things being relative, somewhat larger understanding of God. Abraham is there in scripture not as a model of goodness. But he is there as someone who broke with his culture and opened a door whereby God could move humanity toward a better knowledge of the Creator. Abraham is a kind of spiritual mutation.

By any contemporary standards Abraham would be a monster, and a felon, for this one horrific act alone. And that is not to mention some other unsavory acts like fathering a child by his wife's maid and then driving her and her child out to perish (if God had allowed it) in the wilderness. What was it that Flip Wilson's "Geraldine" used to say? "*The devil made me do it*." With Abraham it was always, "*Yahweh made me do it*."

The problem is that the God of Abraham resembles all too much many boys' own fathers; stern, abusive, testing fathers, fathers that in their religious zeal are willing to offer their own sons. It is a common, though certainly not a universal experience, of gay men. One man I know of, when he came out to his father, was told, "*I would rather have learned that you had died*." That person now leads a so-called "ex-gay ministry" in my denomination. As misguided and dangerous as I believe these programs to be, it is understandable why he is doing what he is doing, when the cost of self-acceptance would be this kind of annihilation in one of the most primary relationships in his life. How does one cope with that level of rejection?

Though not always this extreme, many gay men find the rejection too high a price for their self-affirmation, and they must find a way to identify themselves as not gay. There is also for some of them a payoff. Not only do they avoid the rejection, they are embraced as "evidence" for those churches that hope, and maintain, that homosexuality can be "cured."

The rejection of many gay children by their parents is an abuse directly traceable to the Church. The emotional abandonment of these children is no less terrible than if their parents had abandoned them because they were of an unwanted gender, or skin color, or left-handed. One might mention children who are abandoned because of some birth defect, though homosexuality should not be compared to any defect or abnormality - because in itself it is neither. But it is in the eyes of some parents a defect so great that they disown, abandon, or hide their own child. In a moral society we regard it as an act of enormous cruelty for parents to force their child to live in a closet. News stories sporadically appear of parents who have kept a child locked or chained in a closet for years. These parents, sick as they are, often believe they have acted out of religious or moral conviction. It is also an abuse of a gay child to expect them to live in a closet of secrecy and fear even though the parents or others believe that they are acting out of religious or moral conviction.

In the dream in Christopher Fry's play, Isaac says, "...*surely there's no need for us to be the prisoners of the dark.*" There are still many prisoners of the dark in relation to gay and lesbian persons. There is no need. We may choose, if we will, to step into the light on this issue.

Some persons who have not only made it through high school, and college, or even have a PhD, may never really have graduated from Sunday School, may never have moved beyond the image of God they were given as a child. Some of those images are as inadequate for an adult mind as they are frightening for the child's mind. Theirs is a state of arrested spiritual development. It is not a matter of intelligence of course, or even of knowledge. It is the fear of venturing beyond the schoolyard of their upbringing.

The Sunday school stories, often chosen more for their "action figures" and tales of adventure, than for their meaning, comprise the Bible that many live by. Without citing any of its actual content, conservatives often hold the Bible before their "sisters' and brothers'" faces the way an exorcist holds a crucifix before the eyes of the demon possessed. Mere reference to the object seems to them a countering of evil forces. They seem sometimes not to feel any particular need to deal with much of the actual content.

Most of scripture reflects a "low view" not a "high view" of human sexuality. We've made some progress. Because of the Gospel, because of Jesus, the Psalmist, and some of the prophets, we've come to better understand that God is the God of love, compassion, and justice. That means for us a new sense of our worth. "...*What is man that thou art mindful of him, and the son of man that thou dost care for him? Yet thou hast made him little less than God, and dost crown him with glory and honor.*" (Psalm 8:4-5).

Out of that dignity, rather than denigration, out of that sense of self worth and the worth of others, comes a more healthy, whole, and joyous sexuality. It derives from the celebration of what God has created us to be and the gifts God has given, rather than guilty repression. With that self knowledge and knowledge of God, "good sex" is that which in the long run, as well as the short run, enhances rather than diminishes the human experience. "Good sex" is that which gives greater value, not lesser value, to another person, and which ultimately increases rather than decreases another's and one's own self esteem.

What we can learn from the Gospel is the sanctity and worth of ourselves and others. When that becomes the context of our sexual lives, there is the possibility of finding the full meaning and expression of this great gift. Because of that - not because of rules, prohibitions, intimidation, fear, shame, and threats - we will seek intimacy in the context of love and commitment, in self-giving, self-affirming ways. It will be sex without power games, open and free, not exploitive nor manipulative, but celebrated and enjoyed whether between a man and a woman or between two persons of the same gender.

Since the standard to be upheld is commitment, love, and mutuality, that should apply in homosexual as well as heterosexual relationships. Love, not sexual orientation, is the moral standard. It is also immoral, for many reasons, to try and force those who are not heterosexual to live as though they were for the comfort of those who are.

These standards are not lower but higher than most of what we find in scripture. They are standards based on a concept of human family, love, justice, and self-worth, which Jesus taught. Ironically, it is the Church's contact with the Gentile world, more than the Semitic one, which has influenced us toward this concept of marriage and sexuality. And it is the influences of humanism and individualism, of which many conservatives are disapproving, that have drawn us to the ideal of sexuality being expressed in the context of romantic love. It is an ideal, difficult to fully attain, but one affirmed and celebrated by liberals and conservatives. It is the most predominate theme of our music, literature, and films. On the issue of homosexuality many of those who engage in the debate simply are not talking about the same thing, therefore, they constantly talk past each other. One group is talking about, and thinking about, sex, the other group is talking about love.

There is irony in the fact that society establishes marriage *"for the welfare and happiness of humankind,"* (this language being from a traditional wedding ceremony), and yet many strenuously oppose it for gays. People understand intuitively that it is in the interest of society itself to establish stable families. They, society and the Church, therefore play an essential role as witnesses and generators of those contractual, covenantal relationships, which the state and the Church sanction and bless. Society and the Church, if they could see it, have the very same implied interest at stake in the relationships of gay persons. But rather than honor committed relationships, they denigrate them. If heterosexual marriage were denigrated in the same way by society and the church, it would promote moral chaos.

I just hope the community would not fear. I think that is what it really is - fear of the loss of privilege they have that they don't want anyone else to share. But it is a good thing, it should be shared with everyone and not just a few. We were born this way, and we are a gift of God. We should be able to share equally in all the gifts and all the privileges. And the fear they have is really unfounded because it isn't lessening their ideas or institutions - like marriage. They think somehow we're going to destroy marriage. If marriages are being destroyed, they're being destroyed by people who can't communicate. I don't understand how allowing gay people to be married is a threat to straight marriages. I don't understand that. They need to get over their fear.
                                                              John

In 1999 in California a vigorous debate took place over a proposition (prop 22) on a statewide ballot that defined marriage as only between a man and a woman. It was a preemptive measure to try to prevent any future recognition of same-sex marriages. The proposition passed, a defeat for gays, but the debate was enlightening. As John indicated, there was much fear mongering that if the proposition failed it somehow posed a grave threat to the institution of marriage itself. How would two persons of the same sex being married be a threat to the institution of marriage? Would heterosexual persons cease to marry? Of course not.

It does not change the institution of marriage for them. The argument is a non sequitur, nonetheless many believe it. The only way, (and it is a positive one,) that the institution of marriage would be changed is that fewer homosexual persons would marry someone of the opposite sex as cover for their sexual orientation.

Even stranger arguments were made, as in a conversation David recalls:

> *When Proposition 22 was happening....I was talking to a heterosexual male friend of mine and he said: "Well, I think I'm going to vote against it, but it kind of bothers me a little bit."*
> *And I said "Well what bothers you about it?"*
> *And he said, "It's about the word marriage. That's not what the word means to me."*
> *And I said, "Well, O.K. I understand that."*
> *And he said, "Well, if this happens, what next?"*
> *And I said, "Well, what do you mean, what's next?"*
> *And he said, "Well, if a man can marry another man then what's next? Can I marry my daughter because we love each other, and am I going to marry my dog because I'm very close to my dog"*
> *I said, "Well, you know it's funny you would think like that, because I've never thought of my relations as being on the same level as bestiality and incest."*
> *And he really started stammering and trying to take it back, and I said, "No, don't, it's O.K. But I want you to know that I hope there is no part of you that pities me in any way - for who I am or my life. I'd really hate to feel that coming from you. So if there's any concern, let me tell you, my life is great...My life is pretty much as normal as the one you're aiming at. And to his credit, he handled this beautifully."*
> David

"Love and marriage, love and marriage, go together like a horse and carriage...you can't have one without the other." So the song goes. But a whole lot of folk think that in the case of gays they don't go together, and they mean to see to it that even if they have the one - love - they will damn well have it without the other.

For now, in all but six states and The District of Columbia, they are having their way, but that will change because this has the inexorable force of an idea whose time has come. It will change because behind it is the force of nature itself. How do we prepare them for its coming so that they can receive it with joy? They cannot see it now, but it will not be a loss for them but the gaining of a better world.

Chapter 5

What's Love Got To Do With It?

> "...we had this combination of good god, bad god. If you were good, God answered your prayers, and wishes would come true. If you were bad you were going to get smacked...There was a great deal of guilt and fear with it so feelings were very mixed. It was very bipolar."
>
> Neal

Despite all the statements in sermons and elsewhere that would imply otherwise, God is not mean, petulant, angry, nor vindictive. These are not the attributes of the holy. God does not have an ego problem. People are mean, petulant, angry, and vindictive - some people, or some people some of the time. Projecting these characteristics onto God is the origin of very bad religion. In the ancient world God's wrath may have been the most plausible explanation they could come up with for great natural disasters, but if we have not moved beyond that, the reason lies within ourselves not in God. Moreover we need to get past the primitive idea that we are all sprung from "bad seed." All infants are born innocent, not guilty of anything. Circumstances, and choices, may cause them to become guilty of many things - good and bad. There is sin aplenty in the world, but there is no "original sin," in the sense that an infant is guilty and deserving of death just by entering the world. We die eventually, because that is the nature of life and of creation. It is not a punishment - at least not a punishment from God. There seems to be some acknowledgement of this in a recent Vatican pronouncement that unbaptized infants do not go to Limbo.

The insulting of God is something for which the Church has a specific word - blaspheme. Only it is often the Church itself that is committing this blaspheme by attributing to God that which is evil. There is a long list of those the church has charged with blasphemy, imprisoned, tortured and killed because they committed an unwanted good or spoke an uncomfortable truth. It was, after all, the good which Jesus did that made him to the religious establishment a man to be gotten rid of, the charge of blaspheme being brought against him as the grounds for his trial and crucifixion (Matthew 28:63-66).

If someone wants to attribute to God that which by any rational standard is evil, they will say, *"Ah...but God's ways are not our ways."* God's ways are indeed not our ways, one of our ways being this misuse of scripture to try and stand logic on its ear. But God's ways are not just any way we'd like them to be. The meaning of goodness is not up for grabs. God gives us not only words but the Word that defines what is good. That Word is not the Bible per se, but the incarnation, "the Word," as the author of John's Gospel says, *"...that became flesh and dwelt among us full of grace and truth."* (John 1:14) The prophet Micah says, *"He has showed you, O man, what is good."* (Micah 6:8) Jesus is God's show and tell, God's compelling illustration of goodness. We who call ourselves by His name are intending by that confession to affirm that Jesus' way is God's way. We look to scripture then not to find ways to use it to bludgeon others, but to understand all that we can of Jesus' way. And we should retain even then a great deal of humility for what may remain lacking in both our understanding and our following.

When Jesus says, *"Whoever has seen me has seen the Father,"* (John 14:9) he is saying that if you want to know what God is like, *"watch me, hear what I say and do as I do."* If Jesus is not the bearer of the Christ, then for him to say "the Father and I are one," is delusional. But for those who believe Jesus is Emmanuel - God with us - his point of view, his actions, his teaching, defines for us what is good. For those who identify themselves as Christians there is no higher standard to be found anywhere in scripture or outside of it. The given word - written, and in Jesus the Christ - living, is *"the way, the truth, the life."* (John 14:5-6)

All statements of Christian ethics are theological statements. As statements about right and wrong, good and evil, they are statements about God, the source, and in Jesus Christ the model, of what is good. God's being and God's action defines what is good, but even that is accountable to some rational standard, otherwise individuals can, as it were, design their own religion, and sculpt their own God, based on how they would like reality to be defined. That is the nature of paganism. Without reason there is no accountability in our religion.

Though justification by grace through faith is the theological centerpiece of Protestant and evangelical faith, there are many Christians who ricochet between grace and law. Salvation, they say, is by grace alone; but then it is by law, and their interpretation of the law, by which they judge - and judge quite readily - who is and is not saved. That is duplicity. Are we saved by grace, or are we saved by works? This ambiguity seems rooted in a concept of God as both the forgiving and the punishing father, what Neal called the *"good God/bad God - very bipolar."* According to many who identify themselves as Christians, God condemns and then forgives, but only if one accepts guilt for their very nature (what they identify as "original sin"). It is one thing to repent of one's actions but another to repent of one's own nature especially when that nature is neither chosen nor can be changed. That, of course, is the dilemma for homosexual persons.

To discipline or even punish a child for a wrong and disobedient act does not, of course, mean a parent does not love that child. The discipline is usually because they do love them. But it is quite a different thing if a parent punishes a child, or abandons them, for something that they did not choose and cannot change. There is no way that can be construed as grace, or love.

The gospel preached by some seems clear, God loves us conditionally not unconditionally, even though persons may have no capacity to meet those conditions. That is certainly a gospel without good news. It is like God is saying, *"Here, jump over this twelve foot fence - oh, you can't? Sorry then, that's the only way into my house."* It is not an act of faith to make a fool of God, especially when that is designed to serve one's own bias or prejudice. We can't have it both ways, though many try. Is it grace or law? Many say it is grace, but in fact they live and act as though it is law, or grace for me, law for you. Much of fundamentalism is not simply a version of Christianity, it is a perversion of it, because this duplicity distorts the nature of God as a God of love.

I was behind a shiny new black VW bug one day that had two words in large white old English letters affixed to its rear fender, "Fear God!" Many Christians love the term, and identify themselves as "Godfearing." That too does not always speak well of God. Suppose a young person came to his pastor and confessed to being afraid of his father. One would not expect the pastor to assume that to be a good thing and he or she would surely ask, *"Why are you afraid of him?"* If the response was that the father would get so angry if his son did anything wrong, punish him severely, and continually threaten to throw him out of the house - forever, then hopefully the pastor would be aware that something was very wrong in this relationship.

It would not seem to be a healthy thing that a son feared his father.

It is normal for children to do some acting out and sometimes resist authority, but allowing that they have reasonable respect for their parents' guidance and discipline we would scarcely think it a good thing for our children to grow up being father-fearing and mother-fearing. Why do we think it a good thing to be God-fearing?

Rationally, the one who loves us most is the one we should have least to fear. We hear quoted to us, *"The fear of God is the beginning of wisdom."* The beginning, yes, but not the end of it. It is the beginning of wisdom for a two-year-old to fear the consequences (which certainly should not be brutality) when a parent says, *"No!"* But we are not two-year-olds. We are also told that, *"perfect love casts out fear."* The truth seems to be that in many persons love and fear are deeply related.

If you have a terrible secret which you fear your earthly father might not forgive, imagine the fear of God that one might have of that one who is called Father and from whom no secrets are hid. Those who wanted to raise their children, or others' children, to be God-fearing, have often been remarkably successful.

Some will surely say that I'm being far to literal and that to be Godfearing means to be in awe of God's power and might, not fearful of God's wrath. And they are right. That is what it should mean to be Godfearing. A term that conveys that would be helpful since many persons in fact fear greatly God's wrath, which is not conducive to loving God.

In the interview with the six men, I had expected in their childhood experiences to hear something about fearing God. What quickly came through from virtually each one of them surpassed those expectations.

The first part of my life we were devout Catholics. We had a very rigid picture of God the Father as the old man. The Holy Spirit was always a mysterious force. Jesus was someone who was real but of course in going to Mass, Jesus was crucified every time for your sins. God the Father was basically somebody...(who) was sitting over there in the background always ready to smack you if you got out of line.... You certainly wouldn't want to die having committed certain sins if you hadn't gone to confession. You could end up in purgatory or hell. There was a great deal of guilt and fear with it, so feelings were very mixed. It was very bipolar. It was a message basically meant to keep people under control. Now there were some who were more loving in their actions. We went to Catholic school and we had some great, very loving and positive nuns, and we had some who thought it was their job to inflict the vengeance of God the Father on everyone. If you were really good then you had to suffer a lot like the saints. You were really good if your life was miserable. So everyone is supposed to put up with...all sorts of afflictions... After all Jesus had to do it! They could always point to bloody Jesus up there on the cross with the nails...'"Jesus isn't up there crying, whining, Whack! Whack!"

              Neal

I was absolutely sure God was a man, my heavenly father, and God seemed to me to have a very volatile personality. On the one hand, he loved me and provided all these wonderful things, a roof over my head, food and clothing, and all that. On the other hand, he could take it all away anytime he wanted to. And according to what I was taught, I wasn't worthy of any of these things anyway - so God was sort of doing me a favor just letting me live. This isn't the sort of thing that inspires a lot of self esteem....I knew God was invisible and omnipresent and saw everything I did, and since he could also read my mind he knew all my impure thoughts. This made it very hard to relax. I remember as a kid always walking around saying, "I love God! You bet I love God!" It wasn't so much that I loved God as it was that I was afraid not to.

David

...I definitely had the very clear image of the Michelangelo God touching the finger of Adam, creating life. That's who God was to me. God in the form of Jesus the Son was the one we could actually communicate with. We could get alone with him pretty much. He was the one who came down here and wept with us. He also knew the human condition. God (the father) was far above that. He was too far removed to know what we humans were going through other than knowing we needed to be destroyed. And unlike the term used here, "God smacks you," my impression was, God kills! God wipes out the earth with Noah. When God doesn't like people, he gets rid of them. He has the power to do that....I don't think I was in fear of my life because I really liked the image of Jesus.

Paul

I saw God as, you know, as omnipotent, omniscient, omnipresent - to be feared mostly - when I was growing up. Later, of course, God became more personal; one whom I could trust, lean on, pray to, and who knew my deepest fears....I had friends who were evangelical, who believed in eternal security. In other words, once you accept Christ there's no way for that to be reversed, no matter what you do. And it was, of course, from a Pentecostal background. We did not believe in eternal security. So, therefore, if you did something a minute before you died, or whatever, then you were lost. You would go to hell.

I'd have conversations with my mother and she would be concerned about something; she feared that *maybe she had done something that was rather unchristian. She lived in such fear that she was going to do something that God would be displeased with, and she would be lost. And I said to her, "Mother, why do you live in fear like this? God is not someone who is going to pounce on you for everything you do..." But that's her mind set and she lives in that fearful way.*

Allen

If one conceives that God's love is not only conditional but that God attaches terrible consequences as punishment (such as AIDS) to the unforgiven child then this kind of "father's love" would - among mortals - be identified today as child abuse. In fact many individuals charged with child abuse seem to believe they are imitating God and doing what God requires of them.

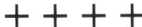

We can only put so much distance between our faith and reason before we must give up on one or the other. Because many persons fear to abandon their faith (even if it is based on a distorted image of God) they choose to give up on reason. Faith, they believe, is essential, reason is optional. What many persons seem to believe is that in the case of religion you can abandon reason whenever it interferes with what you wish or are told to believe. The explanation given is that "*God can do anything*," therefore God can act even in contradiction to God. God being God requires praise for being just and loving, but if what happens is neither just nor loving then one is obliged by their faith to say that never-the-less "*God is good*" and "*God's ways are not our ways.*" No rational standard can then be applied to our faith or understanding of God. In fact reason is treated by some as faithless and subversive in itself.

In my childhood the choice that seemed to be presented was between seeing God as less than all powerful, and therefore unable to control evil; or God himself/herself as one who does or allows evil. Therefore the existence of evil itself seemed to me then evidence that God does not exist, since God would be either less than all powerful and therefore not God at all, or God himself/herself would be evil. This is exactly the theological conundrum presented in Archibald McLeish's play "J.B."

Years later in N.Y. I'd see the original production of that play. At that stage in my journey it stated my theological angst quite well. *"If God is good He is not God, If God He is not good...Take the even, take the odd..."* Looking back, when I was in high school I'd taken the odd, *"...if God, He is not good."* I considered myself an atheist, though I think in retrospect I was on "hold" until someone could give me a more rational answer. Intuitively I knew that if God existed, God had to be good, despite the many who seemed comfortable enough even with the idea of a God that sometimes acted in jealous rage, or was capricious and cruel. Except for being monotheistic, those ideas of God I could see as in no way superior to the Gods of paganism.

Some would respond that theirs is *"faith seeking reason,"* or *"belief seeking understanding."* That seems to unburden them of the need for rational belief. But that can easily be faith seeking opportunity, not reason. It can be faith seeking a rationale for opinions and attitudes one already holds apart from faith - perhaps racism or homophobia. The problem is the same as with any inquiry that begins with a conclusion. All the evidence will be skewed, admitted or omitted, to try and verify the conclusion already reached. They might argue that faith experience itself is evidence that skeptics do not admit.

Faith experience is critical evidence, no doubt, but the issue is really over the individual's interpretation of his or her faith experience. That is very apt to be biased because it is "their experience" subjectively perceived, interpreted, and conditioned by the cultural influences on their lives. They self-certify their own faith experience - but often dismiss the faith experience of someone who does not accept their interpretation of that experience.

Separating our experience of God, which may be whole and valid in itself, from our interpretation of that experience, which may be faulty in many ways, is there a criteria against which we can more objectively judge our ideas about God? God is always more than we can comprehend, but God is never *less* than we can comprehend. So, because we have some idea of what love is, and justice, and truth, we can know that God's love is not hate, God's justice is not injustice, and God's truth is not lies.

There is a lot I learned in seminary that I have no doubt forgotten, and perhaps much that has been stored in some dusty vault in the library of my brain, but there is one thing, perhaps oddly, that is right there in the forefront of consciousness. Perhaps that is because I've always been one for whom reason, even in matters of faith, or especially in matters of faith, is essential. I feel, therefore, a certain affinity with some theologians of the middle ages who were very serious and diligent about the relationship of faith and reason. Not that I reasoned my way to belief, because I know that is futile. I also do not believe that people reason their way to falling in love, but being in love they may seek and find reasons why a particular person makes their heart palpitate whenever he or she is near. Knowing God, being "saved," bears more than a resemblance to the experience of "falling in love." Being saved is falling in love with God. It is in fact falling into the immense, unfathomable love of God.

I've never believed that my reach could come anywhere near understanding who God is, nor even convince me of God's existence. I always pretty much understood that if there were to be a conscious connection between God and myself it would depend on God, not on me. He is the hound, I am the hunted. My joy comes in losing the race, in being caught - a joy I could not have imagined before being caught.

Intellectually, I understand the agnostic's conviction that if God exists he/she would be unknowable. From the strictly human side, that would seem to stand to reason. Does an ant crawling up an elephant's leg comprehend what is thousands and thousands of times larger than he is? With his mere ant intelligence he perhaps perceives at best that he is on something beyond his scope of vision and that seems sometimes to be moving. But the other side of our inability to know God, which also stands to reason, is that if God exists, he/she would have the power to make himself or herself known.

I'm remembering a 'National Lampoon' recording where they depicted God as the 'cosmic muffin,' and that just struck me as such a wonderful comment. God is something we can't even begin to imagine. Hopefully we've gotten rid of the image of the beard, of a human form. God is something so far from my imagination I'm not even going to bother myself trying to put it on paper. As far as my relationship with Jesus and how I picture Jesus, I see him as a wonderful historic figure - more than I ever did before - and not just of history, but the Spirit of Christ living on.

One of the best experiences I've ever had at WHPC (West Hollywood Presbyterian Church) was hearing something from the pulpit that was against everything I'd been taught. Someone was questioning something that was so set in my mind. It was one of our interim pastors who said, "I don't believe this story is true," and it was one of the Jesus stories. And I, and (another member), both of us ran to him following the service and said, "How could you say that from the pulpit?" And being the kind, gentle, loving soul that he was, he said, "Come over for dinner, let's talk." And so we joined him at his house in Silverlake, and we sat over cocktails before dinner and I said, "You can't stand in a pulpit, in my opinion, and say this is not true." And he said, "Of course I can, and you can tell me I'm full of it." And it's the first time I'd ever heard, A: that ministers were fallible (we were never taught that as children) and B: that we didn't have to believe everything our minister told us. And so that was part of the process of clearing my mind of everything I had been taught, and starting all over to discover the Bible; to read the Bible with a fresh point of view, and to discover MY religion, which is what I go to church for every week, for what I perceive to be the truth.

Paul

This last sentence I suppose sounds like all that a fundamentalist fears in 'liberal' Christianity. But what it really means is that individuals must take responsibility for their own journeys, and not turn them over to someone else who claims to have the only map. We must work out our own salvation *"with fear and trembling."*

If the circumstances of someone's life, including their sexual orientation, impels them on the journey, then that orientation is a gift that leads toward an abundance of grace. Truth does not drop down on us from the sky, nor is a spiritual journey one of mere meandering. Before truth is the finding of a criteria that will show us what truth is. Without that we can spend our lives mining fool's gold believing it is the real thing.

In the medieval Church there were those known as Scholastics who endeavored to apply a criterion for defining the nature of God. The most renowned of these scholastics was Anselm (in the later years of his life he was the Archbishop of Canterbury). Anselm maintained that *"he believed in order that he might understand, and that indeed unless he believed there was no possibility of understanding."* This is set forth in his most famous work, "The Proslogium." He held that the criteria of reason to be applied to the nature of God was this: *"God is that than which no greater can be conceived."* In the Zulu language of South Africa god is *"nkul unkulu," "the one bigger than big."* That statement about God, though less academic partakes of the same instinctive understanding and wisdom as Anselm's statement.

When the Bible says, and we say, God is love, that in itself is only a thought, a conceptualization of God, even so, it is understood as being more than an attribute of God, but actually a statement as to the very essence of God. But a thought, an idea, no matter how great in concept is not in itself "reality" until in some way we experience God as love. Love needs an object, and an expression. For the love of God to have an object and an expression, God had to create it. The idea that God was lonely and so created man as companion takes poetic form in James Weldon Johnson's Folk Oratorio, *"The Creation."* But that is art, not a theological statement. To think of God's motive and action in that literal way, to think of it as being linear, i.e. God was love but had nothing to love so he/she created the object of affection, would be to limit God to human categories. But it isn't linear. As God does not have an ending point, so God did not have a starting point. Living in time we see all things as existing in the past, present, and future. Though we cannot conceptualize it, those categories may not be binding on God as they are on us. There never was a time before and then after God created. God creates because that is love's nature. More than that, God enters into God's own creation, steps into time, to show and to express, that love. *"In the beginning was the Word and the Word was with God and the Word was God."* And that Word (logos) *"became flesh and dwelt among us full of grace and truth."*

To experience God as love is a greater reality than simply to believe in the idea that God is love. And for that love to be revealed in flesh (the incarnation of love) is greater than for it simply to be perceived in thought or feeling. Therefore the humanity, and not just the divinity of Jesus, is essential to knowing God as that than which no greater can be conceived. That manifestation in the flesh is to be taken seriously rather than for persons to simply isolate out all that is miraculous and divine about Jesus and thus reduce God - etherealize God - again into an experience of thought or belief only. Jesus shows us what love is by loving us, and love shows us what God is. In John's Gospel we hear, *"God is love and they who abide in love abide in God and God in them."* Love is not something God does, love is what God is. Always, relentlessly, eternally, God is love. Fear not!

The quest for salvation can be like the wounded son seeking the lost or inaccessible father. God is not like that. We do not have to search for God's love or for some magical formula to receive it. God is not the tyrannical father. He is the father of the prodigal son. He runs out to us. He adorns us with honor. He celebrates our coming home.

If we could begin with God - our experience of God - rather than with religion, we might avoid this coming up against the contradiction wherein we feel compelled to abandon either faith or reason. This is a very different road to travel. It engages us more with mystery and with experience that defies both explanation and demonstration. But it allows us to know that which, relying just on ourselves, would be unknowable.

God is love, that's the bottom line, and love is always a mystery from strictly the human side.

God loves you. God will always love you, and God is going to always love you no matter what. And steer clear of people who tell you otherwise, or put qualifications on that and try to manipulate you to do what they want you to do, so they don't have to feel they've made wrong choices in their lives, or that the world isn't operating the way they have it all packed away in their brains. Understand that God loves you dearly.
Neal

Love resides in the self in that well from which arises our tears and our genuine laughter. God is within not without. God is found in a journey inward, not in a journey outward. But there is a paradox - a mystery here. Jesus in his humanity is without, is external to us. In his resurrection and by the Holy Spirit he becomes God within us. We give this paradox, this mystery, expression, if not tangibility, in The Lord's Supper. That which is external, the manifestly real bread and wine, we take within us as God's own presence. The location of God is in the human heart.

The human heart can go to the lengths of God.... Thank God our time is now when wrong comes up to face us everywhere, never to leave us till we take the longest stride of soul men ever took. Affairs are now soul size. The enterprise is exploration into God.
Christopher Fry,
"A Sleep of Prisoners"

If we take that journey inward, make that "exploration into God," then prayer is simply to that inward life what breathing is to our physical bodies. It becomes the milieu in which we live.

+ + + +

What has all this about faith and reason, God within and God without, to do with gay men? When belief is used as a rationale for rejecting the real world, persons allow themselves to reject all the realities related to the lives of gay persons. Religion is conveniently used to defend their homophobia and sometimes their abuse of gay persons. The bias of many Christians against gays is rooted in a wrong concept of God.

When I was in my twenties and lived in New York City I had a friend who had come from Germany to live in the states. He was, as the expression goes, a struggling young artist. He painted somewhat in the mode of German expressionism. He asked me if I would sit for a portrait. Admiring as I did his paintings, I was flattered to be asked. After two fairly long sittings he said that the painting was finished and that I could look at it. I was, of course, eager to see this revelation of myself. What I saw was a somewhat somber painting of a rather lean and intense young man (rather Dostoyevskian). He asked what I thought of it. I said that I would first like to know what he thought of it. I knew his objective as an artist went beyond capturing a mere physical resemblance, which was definitely there. We had a mutual friend, a young woman, whom he had painted several times, and though I thought each looked exactly like her, he was not satisfied that he had captured what he saw and what he knew of her. I was sure he would be equally candid in regard to the portrait he had done of me. After a moment he said, "*It's good. That is you as I know you.*" What was in his mind he had been able to put onto canvas. And he was right, the man in the portrait was an honest portrayal of the very earnest, probably overly intense, young seminarian that I was.

Sometime later, as a gift, he gave me the portrait, and today it hangs on our dining room wall. I look at it from time to time and can see, more than any photograph reveals, the young man I was - and who my friend Wilhelm knew - when I was twenty three years old. The hope of the true artist is to be able to say, *"That's good! So be it, and Amen!"* to his or her own creation.

In Genesis God affirms each stage of creation proclaiming, *"That's good!"* What was in the mind of the maker came forth as the perfect expression of God's will, and power, and love. God's *"Amen"* (which means *"so be it!"*) wasn't just a mutterance, it was a shout roaring through infinity. The trinity (since our earthbound imaginations constrain us to think anthropomorphically about God) gives the maker an *"Amen!"* -- a thumbs up. And to the creature God gives - love. In the liturgy of our life, our *"Amen,"* follows God's own *"Amen!"* God created gay men and women and what God made was intended, and what God made God loved.

There are many who seeing this creation feel something quite other than *"so be it."* Their will is that it not be. But if a loving God looks at their creation and says, *"That's good!"* what other response should be ours than to say, *"Amen, so be it!"*? That is not an *"Amen"* to everything the creature does, for this creature, like all others, often does that which is not good. But God does not put the beloved creation on a shelf simply to admire it. Essential to God's loving is that the creature is given freedom, because bondage is not love. In that freedom the creature often makes wrong choices, choices that diminish the person, that mar the image in which he or she is made. And so there is the stage beyond creation, which is redemption, though perhaps redemption is simply the ongoing stage of creation itself. Where the creature goes, God not only knows, but goes, forever recreating him or her with everlasting love.

Chapter 6

The Bible Battlements

"It ain't necessarily so, It ain't necessarily so.
De t'ings dat yo li'ble to read in de Bible,
It ain't necessarily so."
from "Porgy and Bess"
George Gershwin

"For a man to lie with a man as with a woman, it is an abomination." Slam dunk! There it is. The Bible says it and they believe it. End of story, case closed. It is legitimate, of course, then to ask those persons, and expect them to answer, as to how they feel about dozens of other verses in Leviticus. Those who quote this verse are often conspicuously disinterested in much of what else is in that book, some of which they might find not only contrary to their own views, but considerably at odds with their life style. The Bible, which one hopes would unite Christians, is the source of much that divides them. That unfortunately is very much the case in regard to the Church's relationship to persons who are gay. Some believe that it would unite us if we all just took it literally, though there is no great unity even among those who believe that they do take it literally. What many persons feel is that they are taking it literally because they believe that they accept the "plain meaning" of what they read in the Bible. They do so selectively, however, and the selection can vary according to whatever is a current issue in the Church. In the past they, or their predecessors, accepted the "plain meaning" of verses that

support slavery and the subjugation of women. Those verses on slavery, like verses about not charging interest, or stringent rules about keeping the Sabbath, and many others, are no longer the verses they live by. It's as though verses can be placed either in a "dead file" or an "active file." They may still regard some verses, such as those regarding the subservient place of women, as "active," though not those that support slavery.

What they regard as very active indeed are any verses pertaining to same gender relationships. There are very few such verses though much is made of what is there in spite of doubtful translation, interpretation, or application in regard to real lives and relationships. All this is now much debated in the church. Those who profess to take the Bible literally are also inclined to believe that those who are more progressive or liberal play fast and loose with the scripture, robbing its authority, and selectively interpreting it according to their personal convictions. The issue of the inclusion of gays in the church is fought on this battlefield. It is a war zone, and looks like one. It is a war that is centuries old and has no foreseeable ending.

What many persons often find in scripture, not surprisingly, is what they went looking for. They look for validation of their feelings, and among 66 books, hundreds of chapters, and thousands of verses they are apt to feel that they have found just that. Persons who feel homosexuality is abhorrent look for validation of that in the Bible, and lo and behold there it is - in Leviticus, only instead of saying abhorrent it says it is an "abomination." That word "abomination" seems right on the mark for them. It says what they feel, that homosexuality is terrible and disgusting. Never mind that they readily have the stomach for eating pork which is also an "abomination."

The battle over the Bible rages but seems to go nowhere for the real battle is not in the verses themselves but is in very different ideas as to the origin, interpretation, authority, and appropriation of what are in those verses. The real issue of course is how to read and interpret the Bible with integrity, and that is far more complex and difficult than taking it literally. I once saw a man stand up at a meeting at which Rev. Mel White (author of "*Stranger at the Gate*: *To Be Gay and Christian in America*," and founder of "Soulforce") was speaking and begin his comments by saying that he "*...took the Bible literally.*" Mel responded, rather gently, "*Oh, I hoped that you would take it seriously.*" To take the Bible literally sounds very pious, but in fact it is both false and foolish. No rational person really takes all of the Bible literally, nor should they. It would certainly abuse it to do so.

To take the Bible literally is to tie boulders to it and sink it. For other persons to take the Bible only figuratively, allegorically, or simply as a manual on ethics is to fill it full of helium and float it into space somewhat inaccessible to the real world. Some persons dismantle it to take from it only what they want and leave the rest, and different persons dismantle it to take different things. Some persons turn this sword on its side and use it as a blunt instrument to bludgeon their neighbor. None of these is to take the Bible seriously! None of these takes seriously why it exists and what it is meant to reveal.

The Bible is a sharp - razor sharp - two-edged sword which cuts to the right and to the left, separating truth from falsehood and love from hate or indifference. To take the Bible seriously is to take it as that sword; to take it for that discerning power; to take it in defense of others, not to rattle it against another. To take it seriously is to learn how to hold it with grace, and wield it with power - not power to destroy but power to save.

Who believes that Jesus meant literally that he was a door, or that he was a vine, or even a shepherd? Literalists would likely reply, "*Well, of course not, you have to use common sense.*" But everyone's sense of a thing is not the same, and is not so "common" as to be universal. Using "common sense" means one is interpreting. To allow that any words are allegorical, metaphor, similes, poetic imagery, irony, hyperbole, or that they are culturally and historically influenced, is to engage in interpretation rather than pure literalism. Nor would there be agreement on what parts should be taken literally. Roman Catholics profess to believe that when Jesus took bread and said, *"This is my body,"* and took wine and said, *"This is my blood,"* he was not speaking allegorically, but literally. This literalism was the foundation of the worship of almost the whole Church for over fifteen hundred years, and still is for tens of millions of Roman Catholics. I know of no fundamentalist, who is not Roman Catholic, who takes that literally and believes in transubstantiation.

Many forms of prejudice are, by their very nature, irrational - contrary to reason, contrary to the "inalienable rights" that coincide with being human, contrary to justice, and, from a religious perspective, contrary to the sanctity of creation. Because of that, such prejudice seeks to bypass reason, and most often uses religion to do so. God, some people maintain, is above, beyond, reason. God, being God, can have things any way God wants them, which may just happen to be the way they want them. They fail to acknowledge, or even consider, that if God is a God of love, as they profess to believe, it does not serve faith to believe that God's power circumvents rather than facilitates God's love. These persons tend not to reflect on the possibility that it is not God but they who are unloving. Some individuals who act with prejudice speak almost as though if it were up to them they would be kind and just, but this is the way God made things to be. Therefore they seem to say, *"It isn't my fault if people get hurt; it's God's fault."*

++++

Since many Christians continually argue that their discrimination against gays is simply following what is found in scripture, it seems obligatory to speak here of the infamous verses on which most of them rely. Many Biblical scholars, out of some current necessity because of the church's attitude toward gays, have addressed these verses. It is somewhat amazing that those who use them to condemn gays seem totally disinterested in any serious exegesis of their meaning or application.

There is deeper, more extensive analysis of these few verses (Boswell, McNeill, Helminiak, Wink, Countryman, Rogers, and many others), but because many profess to base their attitudes toward gays on these verses, I want to be sure the reader knows I am not evading these or any other passages. Even to refer to some of them as "passages" is a bit grandiose in that they are, for the most part, single sentences or even single words within a list of words. While the impression is often given, sometimes by those who know better, that the Bible is replete with condemnations of same-sex relationships, and that these references are "perfectly clear," they, in fact, are exceedingly few, and some of them far from clear in their translation and context, and, thereby, their interpretation.

There are, all told, six direct references. Taken chronologically in scripture, most Biblical scholars, conservative and liberal, would now agree that the first one, the Sodom story, found in Genesis 19, has no meaningful application to the issue of same sex relationships being debated in the Church.

When Lot's uncle Abraham sends two angels - who evidently look like ordinary men (they don't have halos, nor wings folded beneath their robes), Lot insists on giving them hospitality in his home and not let them sleep on the street. He recognizes the danger these "strangers" would be in to be so exposed. In the evening all the men of Sodom come to Lot's door, threatening, as the Ku Klux Klan gathering in someone's front yard, and demand that he bring the strangers out that they may "know them." The phrase "to know" is sometimes used in scripture as a euphemism for sexual intercourse. That suggests a threat of homosexual gang rape, though there is not universal agreement among scholars that such an interpretation is the only one possible. But if these words are such a threat it is not about homosexual lust but is about the degradation and intimidation of the alien guests to whom Lot has given sanctuary. No rational person, gay or straight, liberal or conservative, would argue that gang rape, homosexual or heterosexual, is other than evil. This has nothing to do with a homosexual orientation, and certainly has nothing to do with a loving relationship between two persons of the same gender. This story is not about homosexuality. Lot himself seems to assume the men are heterosexual. It is too great a stretch for honest scholars, regardless of their own convictions about homosexuality, to try to draw a meaningful connection between this threatened violence and the love two men may have for each other. Moreover, Lot's offering of his virgin daughters to this mob, presumably to be raped, or as property, would obliterate it as any meaningful commentary on sexual morality.

Interestingly, in the Abrahamic saga it is in the story of Sodom that we see most clearly the alien status of Abraham's family. Lot, an alien himself in this city, gives sanctuary to those perceived by the men of Sodom as foreigners - "illegal aliens." Having Lot in their city is one thing, but when he begins bringing in those of "his tribe," the men of Sodom make it very clear that they are not welcome, threatening to rape them, and degrade them by "using them" like women.

They are perhaps following a principle of ancient culture, one found in Judaism itself (Lev. 25:44-46), that aliens may be made slaves. The threatened rape may have been intended to "take possession" of Lot's alien guests as property and as slaves. Perhaps because Lot's guests are men, who may be perceived as potential heads of families who will move into the neighborhood, they are especially not welcome as free men. In Southern California there have been occasional police actions against persons giving sanctuary to undocumented aliens. In the case of political refugees from Central American countries it was the Church itself that often provided sanctuary.

So what is the "sin of Sodom" if it is not homosexuality? As many scholars have noted, and as is stated in scripture itself, Sodom's sin was inhospitality (Matthew 9:11-15) and a lack of compassion for the poor (Ezekiel 16:48-49). Since many persons are impressed with the term "abomination" in Leviticus, they should note how often that term is used in Ezekiel in decrying the sins of Jerusalem - worse than those of Sodom - which have to do with pride, arrogance, and inhospitality toward the poor.

Perhaps inhospitality sounds like a trivial sin, since we are apt to associate it simply with observing certain social conventions of a proper and polite society. We do not easily comprehend the significance of "hospitality" as an imperative of a particular people's well being, and even their survival. For a Hebrew to give sanctuary to another Hebrew, especially in a strange and threatening environment, was a high ethic. Immigrants in this land might be able to tell us something about what it means to be offered sanctuary and hospitality by their own people in a strange land. During the time of the underground railroad runaway slaves knew what it meant to be sheltered by friends and sympathizers. Jews fleeing the Nazi holocaust understood the consequences of "inhospitality" if turned away by those from whom they sought refuge.

What perhaps we ought to take from this story is that homosexuals are the aliens in the land of heterosexuality. They are the ones regarded as not native, as strangers, as "queer." The Church should be the place where they find hospitality, and sanctuary, but in fact it is the Church - much of it - that exposes them to the threats and abuses of others.

One alternate theory is that the men of Sodom perceived Lot's guests to be divine beings (angels) and believed that sexual contact with them would impart some extraordinary power to them. Although we try to extrapolate some direct meaning out of this story for our own time, if this theory is correct we are looking at something deep in the cultural and superstitious mist of antiquity that does not have any great confluence with our own time or culture.

The second and third of the references are the oft quoted "abomination" verses (*Leviticus 18:22 & 20:13*) which are simply the same thing stated twice within the same portion of the same book (the Holiness Code), the latter reference adding that those who do such things deserve to die. Whoever quotes Leviticus to condemn gays should, I believe, be expected to read that book - every word. It would be a journey for them into a very dark and murky world of fear and superstition. The opening chapters are a grizzly and detailed manual for blood sacrifice to ward off the wrath of a God who seems addicted to the aroma of burning flesh and blood. That is followed by other chapters giving a laundry list of the relatives and in-laws with whom persons should not have sexual intercourse, in case they do not fully understand the concept of incest. (Their own heritage goes back to the incestuous relations of their patriarchal ancestors, who married family members within their own tribe.) Out of this cauldron of fear and superstition some Christians want to extract two viper verses to strike at gays. The Old Testament overall leads us somewhere nearer to light, but where it leads is not into, but out of, this perpetual fire of sacrifice and blood flung at the altar.

The three remaining references are in three New Testament epistles commonly attributed to one author, Paul, though most scholars do not regard *I Timothy* as having been authored by Paul. No other New Testament authors, and Jesus himself, ever speaks a word on this topic. In *I Corinthians 6:9 & I Timothy 1:10-12*, the presumed condemnation hangs on the translation of ,two Greek words, *malokoi* and *arsenokoitai*, both terms being used in I Corinthians, and arsenokoitai used again in the *I Timothy* passage. The translation of these terms is difficult and seems to have been culturally and historically influenced. There were far more common terms for sexual relations between two persons of the same sex when these letters were written. The question then for translators is why the author did not use common rather than these relatively obscure terms (words which could have other meanings), if he was intending to refer specifically to homosexual practice. Though some scholars have translated them with a single term such as "homosexuals," "sodomites," or "sexual perverts," these are interpretative translations which are not the only translations possible. For example, the early Greek fathers of the Church, such as St. John Chrysostom, saw no reference to homosexual practice in the *I Corinthian* passage.

"*Malokoi*" is the plural of "*malakos*" and means, literally, "soft." "*Arsenokoitai*" is a combination of "*koitai*," which means "those who engage in sexual intercourse," and the prefix "*arseno*," which means "male or masculine." *Arsenokoitai* then could mean male prostitutes, which would certainly have meaning to those to whom the author is writing in both *I Corinthians* and *I Timothy*. "Male concubine" was in fact St. Jerome's translation of arsenokoitai in the translation into the Latin known as the Vulgate, the most authoritative translation of the Bible for the Western Church from the late 4th century up to the Reformation. Some scholars believe that *malokoi* and *arsenokoitai* refer to the passive (soft) and active partners in a homosexual relationship. However, that is an interpretation and not merely a translation, and it does not agree with how Biblical scholars far closer in time to the early Church understood these words.

The reliability of the translation of those terms is very much in doubt and thereby an exceedingly thin thread on which to hang the condemnation of gays. In modern versions of scripture the translations seem, in fact, to be based on preexisting prejudice, as earlier translations do not contain the same meanings.

The third New Testament reference is the most relied upon. It is found at the end of the *first chapter of Romans*:

"Therefore God gave them up in the lusts of their hearts to impurity, to the dishonoring of their bodies among themselves, because they exchanged the truth about God for a lie and worshipped and served the creature rather than the Creator, who is blessed forever! Amen. For this reason God gave them up to dishonorable passions. Their women exchanged natural relations for unnatural, and the men likewise gave up natural relations with women and were consumed with passion for one another, men committing shameless acts with men and receiving in their own persons the due penalty of that error."

Romans 1:24-27 (RSV)

It is not dismissive of Paul's serious words here to note several things. The sin he is talking about is not homosexuality but turning away from God. Everyone, Paul believes, has turned away from God, even those who have not heard of Christ, by rejecting the implicit revelation of God in nature. The same sex relations he refers to he sees not as sin itself but as a consequence of sin, manifest in paganism, or perhaps a consequence of the Fall. If it is the latter then homosexuality would fall in the same category as a woman's travail in childbirth, and a man's toiling to make a living from the earth through farming. Today we are apt to consider these "consequences" more as holy than unholy.

Paul's letter is to those he sees as living in the midst of pagan culture. He has, of course, no knowledge of homosexuality as an orientation - as an individual's nature - and so speaks of these acts as unnatural. Paul writes, "*...God gave them up in the lusts of their hearts.*" Paul seems to have no awareness of any same-sex relations as being related to love rather than simply lust. In fact, it is difficult to find in any of his letters that he sees any sexual activity as other than lust. He speaks of two things: impurity (uncleanness) and "dishonoring of their bodies." Paul, before his conversion, had been a zealous Pharisee. He, no doubt, shared the Pharisee's obsession with law and with cleanliness. Some residue of that probably remains in him, including attitudes about homosexual practice as "unclean." The dishonoring, especially for men, referred to putting themselves in the more subservient role of women. For women, the dishonoring referred to not reserving themselves for men.

Paul, writing from Corinth to the Christians in Rome, though no doubt intending a wider audience, is well aware that they live in a very licentious atmosphere for all sexual practice, where even Temple prostitution is common. He uses this as an illustration of the effects of paganism - of turning away from God. He clearly did not intend that illustration to replace his central concern, which is his argument that all persons have sinned and all are in need of redemption. He is building here towards his central affirmation of justification by grace through faith.

To take this passage seriously, it is very important to note that Paul, despite his attitude towards same sex relations, is careful to say his words are not intended as an invitation to judge others, (*Romans 2:1*). That is exactly, however, how his words have continually been used by others against gays.

An interesting feature of the New Testament allusions is that Paul only speaks of sexual practice as allowable, and not sin, for those who haven't the gift of celibacy. They should marry if they must. At most he tolerates the idea saying, "It is better to marry than burn." (*I Corinthians 7:9 KJV*). That is not a great endorsement or celebration of marriage. Because he had an eschatological view of history, he saw no need of further procreation; since the world would imminently be coming to an end. He seemed, basically, to regard sexual union as unnecessary and tended to view it as an unfortunate, if not unseemly, concession to the flesh, and an encumbrance to the evangelical mission. That no doubt set a tone for much of the Church's anti-sexual attitudes.

Under even cursory examination, it is clear that the six references, often referred to by gays as the "clobber verses," never refer to, nor seem to conceive of the possibility of same sex relationships in the context of love and commitment. In part, this is because love was not the basis for even heterosexual relationships - ownership was. A man could have relations with those who "belonged" to him, and with as many as belonged to him, including slaves. Abraham conceived by Hagar, Sarah's maid, and Jacob by the maids of both Leah and Rachel. As wives were the property of their husbands, so their maids were their property as well. In the Roman world an extension of that was that men could have sexual relations with slaves and wards, male or female, because they "belonged" to them. That is not to say that love never entered in and that men did not love their wives. But marriage and sexual relations being based on romantic love is a much later, and largely Western, concept. In much of the world it still is not the basis for the establishment of families.

The current turmoil in the Middle East, has served to bring this part of the world, and Middle Eastern culture, into sharper focus for many Americans who have tended to know little of it. Middle Eastern culture, religiously and in other respects, is, of course, diverse and varies from region to region, country to country. We have, however, begun to see more what patriarchal culture looks like and how individuals and families function in such a society. This should help us to see more clearly the cultural setting of much that is in the Bible, especially the Old Testament. The stories we read in scripture fit far more into this picture than into "Western" society.

Some would like to bring in other possibilities for using the Bible to condemn homosexuality using "arguments from silence," that is, arguing that the Bible infers something by what it *doesn't* say. For example, because it never says anything in favor of same-sex relations, some infer that is condemnation of them, or that homosexuality is wrong because God made Adam and Eve, not Adam and Steve. Though if God made us all, God did make Adam and Steve, and Ada and Eve.

Arguments from silence are a notoriously unreliable way of exegeting scripture. Using that method, one can construct virtually anything they want scripture to say. Protestants have long been dubious regarding those Roman Catholic Marian doctrines, the immaculate conception and the bodily assumption, that are "inferred" from what the Bible doesn't say. Jesus never said one word about same-sex relationships. What should we infer from that silence?

Persons on either side might infer whatever they like, but, in fact, silence is silence; it's not a blank check for one to fill in however they like. Since Jesus condemns many things, particularly of the self righteous, his silence on this subject would at the very least indicate this issue was no where near the core of his message and teaching.

Much as some might claim that the Bible gives us clear direction for our sexual lives, it should be conspicuous to any serious reader of the Bible, Old and New Testaments, that the sexual ethics we generally affirm are higher, not lower, than those based on property rights and patriarchy. Despite the abuses and violations of these ethics that occur, most people believe that commitment, consent, and mutuality, not to mention love and tenderness, should belong to our sexual lives. None of these was a necessary part of what was sexually allowable in the Bible. Adultery was about property rights. Fornication was about "not handling the merchandise" unless you were going to buy it (offer the father, or male possessor of this property, a dowry in exchange for her as his bride).

There seems sometimes to be a correlation between the degree to which persons beat the drum for the authority of scripture and the degree to which they actually treat scripture with less intellectual integrity than a popular work of fiction. Many speak about it so loudly and with such conspicuous piety as cover, it seems, for themselves and for others who pick and choose among its thousands of verses, putting them together in whatever combination, and with whatever translation and interpretation that serves their bias.

They also flatten out revelation so as to treat any single verse or word, for that matter, as having the moral weight of any other verse or word in scripture. That way they can always have available a handful of "gotcha" verses. When they want to judge the actions of others, they pull out one of these verses and lay it on someone as if to say, "gotcha!" To put it another way, they load up their Biblical gun with these "bullets," always ready to fire one in their self-appointed role as a "defender of the faith."

But perhaps a better analogy is that some persons use the Bible as one plays a harp. The music they get depends on what strings they strum and pluck. There is music to be heard from scripture (see Chapter 12), but not every song is God's song.

Through most of her history the Church's final authority was not the Bible but the Church, specifically the clergy in its hierarchical order. What was authoritative was the interpretation the Church gave to the Bible, what she declared as canon and not canon, and what she chose by Papal decree to add to that.

The Reformation put the Bible in the hands of the laity as well as the clergy. The Bible itself was declared to be the Church's ultimate authority, though there might be a thousand interpretations of it. The major Protestant denominations tried to put some perimeters on interpretation through its Confessional statements, but the fundamentalist churches in time cut themselves loose from these, and developed their own confessional standards. In my denomination there are some who are trying to do that again with something they call "the Confessing Church Movement." Though the Reformed tradition has itself always been a confessing Church movement, the fundamentalists within it want now to narrow the confessions, edit them, or prioritize them, according to their particular theological bias.

One scriptural concept that fundamentalists and evangelicals regard as essential is that believing and accepting Jesus Christ as savior is the only means of salvation. When Jesus said, "the Father and I are one...," I understand that as meaning that to look at this person, Jesus Christ, and know what He is like is to know what God is like, and how this man loves is how God loves us. That does not mean that unless persons in their own situation know of Jesus and can experience him as we do, they cannot experience God's love as truly and as deeply as we do. We can point to Jesus but also trust that God has ways of making his/her love felt and known. If that were not so, no one before Jesus, and the crucifixion and resurrection, could experience salvation

When Paul speaks to the men of Athens who gather round him to hear of this "foreign religion" (*Acts 17:16ff*) he speaks to them of "a God unknown." Implicit in his message is that God addresses the hearts even of those to whom the name is yet unknown. There is the same implication in *Romans 1,* a passage, so commonly, and inaccurately, used against gays and lesbians. Here Paul says that persons are without excuse because God is revealed in God's creation even apart from the explicit revelation in Jesus Christ. If they are accountable, then they are also accepted in receiving the revelation that they have. That stands to reason, for anyone to whom reason matters.

Instead of absolutes, discovering the nature and will of God, for me, is a journey. That journey is more theologically productive than mere study and reflection, though such study and reflection may be part of that journey. Historically, journey was the catalyst for much of the scriptures, old and new. Journey was certainly the source and inspiration of most of the Abrahamic saga. The whole of the Old Testament comprises a story of extraordinary spiritual development growing out of the journeying of a particular people; their migration, captivity, exodus, exile, return, and dispersion. Periods of prosperity and ease tended toward stagnation and were for them the least productive in their spiritual development.

Following Pentecost there was another dispersion, and journey, among those who carried the story of the life, death, and resurrection of Jesus, and this included journeying across geographical and cultural boundaries. The journal of that journey is the New Testament.

If we begin with that we can look back through scriptural history and see it as it is - one of unfolding story. That is a very different perspective than rummaging through scripture to find whatever one can to support existing convictions, convictions drawn not out of scripture but out of one's own environment. Scripture has often been used by those of a particular society to validate themselves. Scripture, though it reflects more the culture in which it is written than our own, is used to endorse our convictions, our life style, and our prejudices. In turn we claim the authority of scripture, and the particular interpretation of scripture that validates who we are and where we are within the culture. There is circular reasoning going on in all of this. When scripture is made self-serving, one can expect that it is not going to be used by most persons to challenge the status quo.

If we accept what John says, "...*God is love, and he (those) who abides in love abides in God, and God abides in him (them) (I John 4:16 RSV),*" we come at our understanding of God, our external knowledge of God, through that internal knowledge, through that experience of God. So then if we look at Abraham, or Moses, or David, any of the prophets, or the disciples we see them in the context of that unfolding story. We don't have to defend everything they did but only see how it is part of how God is revealing God's self.

Everything we see then must be grounded in that prior knowledge and experience of God as love; an experience that is not only our own but a collective experience we share in the fellowship of the Church. It is an experience that belongs as authentically to many gays as it does to others. We begin with the Word (Jesus Christ) to interpret the word, not the other way around. We build on a solid foundation, on rock, on Peter's insight that this man, Jesus, is God's self revelation. This is flesh and blood - that is, something that external knowledge has not revealed, but something inward, the Spirit of God. It is knowledge that is not intellectual, but knowledge in the heart. We will be given hearts of flesh for hearts of stone. Flesh is good!

Our knowledge of God, which becomes knowledge of ourselves and others, resides in our experience of God and in other's experience of God, the same as our knowledge about all other things. Ultimately anything that is known goes back to something empirical, to something experienced. To understand our experience, we look to where it resonates with others and with history. As God is love, our primary experience of God is of being loved. It is an experience that we can joyfully share with others who experience God's love as we do. It is an experience we can share with others, because we know that they, too, can experience God as love.

Only when we come back to knowing that God is love will we understand fully that God's love is inclusive, and what is in the heart of one is as valid as what is in the heart of another. We are not made the judges of that.

You know if parents have five children and they are addressing one of those children about something that has happened, and others of the children pipe up with their own ideas or accusations or threats, the mother or father will turn to them and say: "*You stay out of this. This is not your business.*" We need to hear that when Paul says, "*judge not that you be not judged.*" How inclined we all are to jump in and judge our siblings, but we've no permission to do that. To make ourselves the judge is to try and usurp the prerogatives that belong to God alone. It is an attempt to overthrow God and put ourselves upon the judgment throne. Doing that we act as though all gays stand before us as defendants. They do not!

Chapter 7

Hearts of Flesh

> "It's my contention that a man who is capable of sweating fantastically for the flesh is also capable of sweating fantastically for the Spirit."
>
> Jack Keruac, on the character of Neal Cassady in, "On the Road."

    I met Job one evening in a piano bar in Chicago. After several days of attending a large ecumenical conference in DeKalb, for gay and lesbian Christians and those engaged in ministry with them, I decided to spend a couple of days in downtown Chicago. It is a city I had usually seen only from the air when landing or taking off from O'Hare. I had arranged to meet a friend for breakfast at the Chicago Trade Mart where he is a trader. I spent the remainder of the day at the magnificent Chicago Art Institute. Looking for something interesting to do in the evening I decided to go to a nearby piano lounge I found advertised in a brochure in my room. When I arrived, the pianist/singer who held forth there nightly was being celebrated on her birthday by those who were clearly regulars in this establishment. This immediately conveyed a pleasant sense of family about the place. Also on that particular night, a Monday I believe, a young man, named Job Christianson, who was starring in a local production of "Joseph's Technicolor Dreamcoat," had come to sing. The theatre being dark on Monday, Job, a very welcome guest artist, had come here, apparently because he simply loves to sing and likes this more intimate contact with an audience.

Introducing various songs, Job would tell anecdotal things about his own life, including the fact that he is gay. Toward the close of his first set of songs he said, *"I want to share something with you out of my spiritual roots."* And then he sang, "His Eye is On the Sparrow."

"I sing because I'm happy. I sing because I'm free, for his eye is on the sparrow, and I know he watches me."

As he went around the room during the break visiting for a few minutes with virtually every individual there, I introduced myself and told him that I had heard Ethel Waters sing that song (the title of her autobiography) in the Old Madison Square Garden during Billy Graham's Crusade in the late fifties.

Also during the break Job had asked if people had song requests to write them on a napkin and place them on the piano, and if he knew the songs, he would sing them. When he returned from the break and went through quite a number of such requests he said, *"You all want to hear hymns."* I was deeply impressed how he had, perhaps surprising even to him, touched upon a well of spiritual hunger.

Back in Claremont I contacted him on e-mail to see if I might interview him for a book I had in mind, inspired in part by that evening in the piano bar. He was quite willing to respond. I received the following response to my asking him what relationship he felt there was between his sexuality and his spirituality.

I believe that sexuality is spirituality and vice versa. They are one and the same. When we feel sexual I think it is our spirit energized and buzzing. The whole "being saved" bit in the fundamentalist religion is like (that)...and my mother explained it to me that way.

This wasn't the sort of response I had expected, and seemed a bit "off the wall." I might easily have dismissed it as not useful to what I was writing, though I was impressed that it was one given in such an open and non-defensive way. As I reflected on what Job had said it began to seem less strange, and contained insight that had eluded me. I found myself remembering how often others, in attacking gay sexuality, had said that the sexual act (meaning their sexual act) is holy, and that it is spiritual as well as physical. This is often said as though it were self evident that a sexual union between two persons of the same gender could not be "holy," could not be spiritual.

Perhaps Job's statement, I thought, contains a remarkable insight, that sexual union with someone you love is as apt an analogy as any other for spiritual rebirth or awakening. All the descriptions of this experience are of necessity in the form of analogy, none of which fully defines the experience. One reaches for that which comes as near as possible to conveying the inexplicable in the explicable.

Perfect analogies of this experience, which is like no other, do not exist, though scripture offers us many. The term "born again" is itself an analogy. What many religious persons I suspect would not like in Job's statement is that it removes the antagonism between flesh and spirit. This dualism is part of how they understand the relationship of God to the world, the holy vs. unholy sinful flesh. After all, though we seem out of embarrassment to not often go there, we have in scripture, "The Song of Songs." How often are you apt to find this in the liturgy of a Sunday morning? *"Hark! My beloved! Here he comes, bounding over the mountains, leaping over hills. My beloved is like a gazelle or a young wild goat; there he stands outside our wall, peeping in at the windows, glancing through the lattice..."* (Song of Songs 2:8-9) This is a remarkable image, of the beloved one "peeping in" on our nakedness.

Is this our naked souls? And there are many other verses in this book with which some persons would likely be even less comfortable. To explain the inclusion of "The Song of Songs" in the canon - which never once mentions God - the Church has traditionally said that this erotic love poem is an analogy of the relationship of Christ to the Church (though the book is Old Testament rather than New Testament). That seems not really very different than Job's statement.

For many, if not most gays, men and women, the struggle to be reconciled to their sexual orientation has inevitably meant reckoning with their religious orientation. Some have accepted their religion's imposition of shame for their sexual orientation and have committed themselves to celibacy, heterosexual marriage, or to so-called "ex-gay ministries." Others have tried to make their peace by simply rejecting their spirituality, which is associated for them with the abuse they have experienced coming from religion. Some have found the distinction between religion and spirituality and have been able openly to hold on to the latter. Others have refused to give in to religion and have remained within its institutional forms in order to sensitize and reform it. This last category is a small one, and is the one to which I am most related. The others, a great majority, seem to have given up on the institutional church, if not on their personal religious beliefs, and it is easy to understand why. Those who have not given up have shown remarkable forbearance and perseverance.

What becomes evident with any honest observation, not just of others but even of oneself, is that with sexuality and spirituality the one cannot be truly divorced from the other. Therefore, many gays as they grow up find that their sexual orientation and the religious orientation are on a collision course. And that is ironic because to trace back one's spirituality and one's sexuality, as two streams, would be to find that they arise from the same spring - the same source, as Job suggested in the response he sent to my question. Saying they are the same thing may strike many as an overstatement, but the two are more kin than foe. Many, however, especially gays, have difficulty keeping the two together, and have felt compelled to choose between their spirituality and their sexuality. The church has often encouraged, if not caused, that divide. Having a pastoral role in affirming the marital relationships of parishioners, much of the Church extols intimacy between married heterosexual persons, but it does so in such a way as to denigrate it in those who are denied the right to marry.

Many persons are perhaps never fully recovered from the sense that sex is somehow "dirty," and therefore how could one possibly find any comparison to the sacred experience of spiritual transformation in something as earthy as sexual union. This attitude is evident in the tendency to characterize any sexual humor as "dirty jokes." Even though there are some - adolescent in age or attitude - who mistake vulgarity for humor, sex itself, being a universal and significant part of life and one that touches on many aspects of human experience, is quite a legitimate and fruitful source of genuine humor. Even married persons, especially some "religious" ones, are apt to have some residue of that feeling of sex being "dirty." This is despite the fact that society and the Church have blessed their "enormous bliss," and even though pleasure rather than procreation is usually its goal.

Job's statement caused me to recall a little adventure some of my college friends and I had many years ago on a weekend excursion to Seattle. We were students at Whitworth College in Spokane. It was a Presbyterian College and very evangelical. We decided one evening to go to hear "Brother Ralph," a popular radio evangelist in the northwest, who broadcast his services from a former movie theatre in downtown Seattle. We sat in the balcony and had a good view of the stage.

After the praise singing, the hellfire sermon, and the altar call, came the healing service. As voices joined in the invitational hymn, worshippers lined up on the stage steps ready to have Brother Ralph lay is healing hands on them. Most, as I recall, were women. He would ask what their ailment was, then one hand would be placed on their shoulder and the other thrust rather violently against their forehead pushing them slightly backward as he addressed the demon of their infirmity and cried out, "in the name of Jesus - be healed!" There were persons assigned to catch them and lower them to the floor as they fell "*stricken under the Spirit*." What you did not catch from hearing this on the radio is that some of these women would writhe in apparent ecstasy there on the stage floor. I felt like I was witnessing some deep convergence of Spirit and flesh which I had never seen in my Presbyterian Church. I was both fascinated, and oddly, embarrassed, as though I were witnessing something almost sexual.

It is precisely the closeness of our spirituality to our sexuality that scares many, and that may be especially true for gays. It seems like the Gospel is boobie trapped. If they taste its joy, they ingest guilt with it. But they are already hooked on joy, and so begins for many the endless cycles of joy, guilt, recrimination, self-hatred, repentance, and forgiveness. And then because they cannot escape nor affirm who they are sexually, it cycles all over again, driving many of them to therapists, some of them to suicide, and driving most of them out of the Church, which has become for them a very toxic environment. It was such an environment for Gerald:

A problem I always had from my background was the question as to where the intellect fell into all of this. For me, the spirit was the emotional component of the intellect. My background was that the flesh was dirty, ugly, sinful, and weak....you had this spirit/flesh dichotomy. It was something you just had to bear up with until you got transported into the spiritual world, to heaven. That kind of fell away for me with my coming out. I had to accept my sexual physical self (though) sometimes I still think of myself as a talking head. I think what I've gotten (out of my experience as gay) is a closer sense of oneness (of spirit and flesh).

In the Presbyterian Church, part of the original language used to disqualify persons for ordination as Minister of the Word and sacrament (i.e. clergy), elder, or deacon - was if they were "self-affirming." How do you strike more deeply against a persons' psychological well being than to tell them that because of something intrinsic to who they are they should not affirm themselves? The terms that many Christians would set are these, "We will accept you if you don't accept yourself." Those are more than unacceptable terms for reasonable persons. They are cruel, abusive, and unbearable conditions. If you love someone of the same gender, and you are in a committed relationship with that person, to be expected to repent of that is as irrational as it would be to ask a man to repent of loving his wife.

We are accustomed to identifying three spheres of being: body, mind, and spirit. Though only the body is tangible, wholeness resides in maintaining and nurturing all three, and indeed the three are not nearly as divisible as we might think. The popular image of the dead coming back as see-through ghosts, or that angels are disembodied spirits, conveys the idea that spirit can exist apart from flesh. An interesting feature of the Sodom story is that the "angels" who visited Abraham under the Oaks of Mamre were not disembodied spirits, they were flesh *(Genesis chapters 18 and 19)*. Initially the visitors - they are referred to in the plural - are identified as "the Lord," but when they appear in Sodom at the beginning of Chapter 19 they are identified as two angels. Abraham had washed their feet, and fed them. And flesh is exactly how they were perceived by all the men of Sodom *"young and old, without exception,"* who stormed Lot's house. The Christian tradition of trying to separate spirit and flesh, body and soul, is not only a false hope but a dangerous enterprise. We are not and cannot be "disembodied" spirits, renouncing the flesh. We are embodied ones, spirit embodied in flesh. We know that the old dichotomy of flesh and spirit is false when we feel that what joins them are the tendons of the heart.

Human sexuality, which resides in the whole being of every person, is the soul reaching out to embody the spirit in the flesh. The dichotomy, the animosity of spirit and flesh, is removed when our sexuality becomes the embodiment of the spirit. Lest that sound too mystical, it means that our sexuality is perfected in relationship, in connecting with another in caring and reciprocating ways. The spirit without the flesh is like sound unheard, beauty unseen, touch not felt, taste and smell unknown. In her one woman show, "The Search for Intelligent Life in the Universe," Lily Tomlin poses and then answers the question, *"Will there be sex in heaven?" "Yes,"* she says, *"we just won't feel it."* That pretty well nails the false dichotomy of flesh and spirit.

The converse of spirit without flesh, the flesh without spirit, is a kind of pornography. Sex without relationship, sex that simply relates to the other as sexual object, is pornographic. This perhaps is the meaning of Jesus' admonition that if you look at a woman and lust after her you have committed adultery in your heart *(Matthew 5:28)*. Ironically perhaps, many religious persons view gays - not with lust of course, but merely as sexual objects. They strenuously resist considering the relational context of their sexual lives, though that is essential to how they expect their own sexuality to be understood. The great significance of the film *"Brokeback Mountain"* is that it compelled the viewer to see two gay men as both spirit and flesh. The objectifying of gays provokes some of them to parody other persons' caricature of them. Some of the more outlandish things one sees in a Gay Pride Parade are a sort of playful mocking of their critics. But I fear their critics don't get it.

There are other ways, of course, other than our sexuality, through which we endeavor to incorporate the spirit in the flesh. In our worship we call this a sacrament. Consider the meaning of The Lord's Supper. We seek an incorporation of ourselves with Christ, and each other, not just in spirit but in flesh. The meaning of this in the Roman Catholic Mass is a very literal kind of incorporation. Also consider the many ways in which Jesus used touching and being touched in his healing and his relationships: touching the leper, the blind man, foot washing, the Passover Meal. During that meal we have the specific mention of John leaning on his chest. And even Judas betrays him with a kiss (suggesting that such greeting between Jesus and his disciples was common). There is a surprising physicality in the Gospels. It is particularly surprising when one considers that they were written down decades after the events took place. The memory of touch is unique and lasting.

What is so remarkable about the Gospels is what the writers regarded as relevant and what they regarded as irrelevant. They will include an extraordinary detail, like Jesus drawing in the sand, or making spittle to put on a blind man's eyes, but they never describe Jesus physically in any way. We do not know if he was short or tall, was slightly built or of large frame. We know nothing really of his facial features. All the paintings of Jesus, in which he is usually readily identifiable, are totally made up. Almost any other biography would begin with such physical description as disclosing something about the person. Think how much we associate Lincoln's rugged face with who he was and what he did. That "great omission" in the Gospels is particularly conspicuous in relation to the resurrection appearances.

Many mystics tried extreme measures to subjugate the flesh while nurturing the spirit. This led to an obsession with the flesh, and sin, that could easily spiral in the opposite direction of its intent. That seemed to happen to Martin Luther. As an Augustinian monk, the more he punished the flesh for the sake of the spirit, the more he was obsessed with his failings, which led him away from, rather than toward the experience of grace and the liberation he sought. He could not achieve by his self-punishment the separation of spirit and flesh he so earnestly sought. There are intimations perhaps that Paul went through a similar struggle.

I do not understand my own actions, for I do not do what I want, but I do the very thing that I hate. Now if I do what I do not want, I agree that the law is good. So then it is no longer I that do it, but sin that dwells within me. For I know that nothing good dwells within me, that is, in my flesh. I can will what is good but I cannot do it, for I do not do the good I want, but the evil I do not want is what I

do. Now if I do what I do not want, it is no longer I that do it, but sin which dwells within me.
(Romans 7:15-20)

We do not know to what specifically in Paul's life this agonized statement refers. It may or may not have been related to his sexuality. It nonetheless perfectly portrays the internal struggle of the person religiously conflicted because of his or her sexuality, and that includes many who are gay.

In scripture, Paul and other writers made the connotation of flesh - evil, yet sometimes it has a very positive meaning in scripture: the flesh that covers the dry bones in Ezekiel's vision *(Ezekiel 37:1-10)*, *"I will give them hearts of flesh for hearts of stone."* What greater affirmation of flesh can there be than the incarnation itself? *"And the Word became flesh and dwelt among us full of grace and truth." (John 1:14).* Yet, as I discuss in Chapter 8, it is difficult for many Christians to truly accept God in the flesh.

It is in our flesh that we feel pain and pleasure. Flesh is the medium of our experience of being human. Our "hearts of flesh" are hearts that feel, hearts that care, hearts that are open, vulnerable. To quote Christopher Fry from his verse drama "*A Sleep of Prisoners,*" in a dream of Shadrach, Meshach, and Abednego in the fiery furnace one of the characters says, *"It's flesh were in, and a fine old dance it is."* Many gays, finding their flesh inescapable, and unable to affirm themselves, have found the choreography of that "*fine old dance*" a very difficult one. We aim for the spirit, but we are in the flesh, and sometimes it is the only dance we know.

Gay men have fought this battle of trying to separate spirit and flesh, again and again, some of them in so-called ex-gay ministries, sometimes it is only to find that self hatred and shame do not result in greater spirituality and healthy sexuality, but a basic disconnect within themselves that leads toward spiritual disintegration and sexual compulsion.

The Church, much of it, is loathe to admit any of the complexities of human sexuality or to examine the relationship between sexuality and spirituality. For centuries it was willing to define sexuality only as the divinely given impulse toward procreation. The Catholic Church today, though certainly not all its members, still holds close to that in the moral requirement that all sexual unions be open to conception.

If sexuality were intended only for procreation then God, if we believe God can do all things, could have created us in such a way that our sexual impulse comes into play only when procreation is the wanted and expected outcome, as is the case with some species. The medical plan for Presbyterian ministers provides, if prescribed, ten Viagra pills per month. Obviously our denominational medical plan is allowing for a drug that treats not an illness but a human urge which the Church regards not just as legitimate but in the interest of supporting heterosexual marriage. A couple celebrating its 50th anniversary may therefore, with the blessing of society and Church - and the medical plan, have "had sex" hundreds if not thousands of times, and have produced only two, three, or four children. At the same time, others because they never married, or because they were gay and not allowed to marry, should never, according to the Church, in the same fifty years, or ever, experience sexual intimacy. At the very least, that portrays God as an unkind creator.

It makes little theological sense to believe that God burdens human beings all their lives with an impulse to which they are forbidden over a lifetime to respond. Moreover, that burden bears a kind of irony if the impulse is one inextricably related to one's spirituality.

The sexual unions of married persons is obviously far in excess of what is needed to preserve the specie, and today it threatens the earth with overpopulation. If procreation were the only moral justification for sexual intimacy then such union for most men and women over forty-five would be immoral.

Persons who choose the monastic or convent life try perhaps to transpose their sexuality into their spirituality. On a radio program I produced when I was in seminary, called *"Theologs Dialogue,"* I once interviewed several Roman Catholics regarding their vow of celibacy. One of the nuns cheerfully declared that her sexuality was one of the most important things in her life. She went on to explain that her sexual "energy" was directed into her ministry. How successfully persons can do that over time remains a question. Many of those who describe themselves as "ex-gay" endeavor to be celibate if they do not marry. Priests, monks, and nuns, who generally regard celibacy as a "calling" and not a mere abstinence, may have some greater success in fulfilling that calling by living in the context of a supportive community of other celibate persons. Evidence, however, seems to be that even in such a supportive environment, over the long haul, many have found that calling extraordinarily difficult. It is even more so for many gays who are not in a supportive environment but isolated and closeted.

At its best, sexual intimacy is an experience beyond empathy. Since giving and receiving are so often positions related to power, such intimacy has the potential of transforming a power struggle into one of mutual empowerment. One gives pleasure in receiving it and receives in giving it. Since a loving sexual relationship may transform power relationships at the personal level, the antiwar slogan, *"make love not war,"* has some deep logic behind it.

Being a convergence of body, mind, and spirit, lovemaking (and not all sex, of course, is lovemaking) our sexuality can be a paradigm of Christian living. But it can, and often does, miss that mark. Like most other things in our life, it is seldom perfect. Even within marriage, of course, sex may be manipulative, exploitive, conflicted or shame based. The Church, not wanting to peer into their bedrooms, extols the sexual intimacy of heterosexual couples. It, however, often does so in what seems to be a "left-handed" slap at non-heterosexual, gay sexuality, and in the current debate over gay marriage, is self-serving and politically motivated.

Homosexuals, according to the Catholic Church, are *"inherently disordered."* Laura Schlessinger, the radio self-proclaimed "therapist," defines them as *"biological errors."* According to James Dobson, former head of "Focus On the Family," *"homosexuality is a gender identity disorder."* And in the "ex-gay" reparative therapy movement they are seen as victims of *"sexual brokenness."* Some persons tend to believe that if they can put a theological, biological, or psychological name to this phenomena, they have adequately defined "the problem." But in the end, all of these terms *"inherently disordered," "biological errors," "gender identity disorder"* or *"sexually broken,"* while sounding more sophisticated or compassionate, mean the same as the more common, straightforward, and ungarnished street terms - "queer" or "pervert." Gays themselves sometimes refer to themselves as "queer" to undercut the self-deception of those who want to perfume their language with more high sounding terminology.

Gay liberation does not inherently advocate, as some seem to assume, a licentious attitude or lifestyle. What though is intended by the term "*gay liberation?*" Is this a dismissal of Biblical admonitions against adultery, and the Biblical "f" word, fornication? Are these the strictures from which gays seek to be "liberated?"

For those in committed relationships, the term adultery has the same meaning for gays as for heterosexual couples, and that meaning is somewhat greater than it was for many of the Biblical writers. For them it was primarily a violation of their patriarchal system. A man caught in adultery was guilty of stealing another man's property. This, thankfully, is not all that is meant by adultery today in this culture. Since women are not to be regarded as property, adultery is the violation of a sacred, but egalitarian, covenant. It is unfaithfulness. In the Old Testament, for a king who had several wives and many concubines, the idea of "unfaithfulness" is moot. When Nathan charged David for his adultery with Bathsheba (*2 Samuel 12:1-14*), it was not an issue of his unfaithfulness to his wives, but of his having taken another man's property. Today, in this culture, the breaking of the covenant of marriage is devastating to that relationship and deeply injurious to the family affected by that act.

Looking at the Gospels, one ought to ask when hearing the story of the woman caught in adultery (*John 8:2-11*), where is the man with whom she was "*caught*"? If she was "*caught*," she was not caught alone. If she was committing adultery, so was he, even if he was unmarried. Remember King David was charged with adultery not for his unfaithfulness to his own wife or wives, but because he had sexual relations with another man's wife. Why was the crowd not about to stone him to death? Could there have been a double standard? More precisely, in this story, could there *not* have been a double standard?

In the story we are given the remarkable detail that Jesus squatted down and drew in the sand. But we are not told the meaning of that. Perhaps the Gospel writer assumes the reader will know. A popular idea, seen in the old original "*King of Kings*" movie, is that Jesus wrote in the sand the sins of the woman's accusers. That I think is a stretch. More likely it seems is a far simpler explanation. Jesus drew a line in the sand. On one side of that line was Jesus and the woman, on the other side were her accusers and would be executioners. It poses the question for us of what side of that line we will choose to stand on in relation to gays. Many Christians, it seems, choose to stand on the side of the accusers.

Fornication is a charge often brought against homosexuals. Does advocating for gays mean advocating for "fornication," for promiscuity, for "sleeping around?" There is promiscuity among many gays, as there is among many heterosexuals. The Church condemns this as though it has an egalitarian position, denouncing this activity among heterosexuals as well as homosexuals. But clearly attitudes are not nearly as egalitarian as the language. This behavior among some gays is treated with greater abhorrence and less tolerance by many than the same behavior among so-called straight persons.

Whether such activity is by homosexuals or heterosexuals, it is not something inherent to either orientation. But one thing is certain, clear, and observable, a society that does not honor committed relationships pushes persons in the direction of noncommitted relationships. We get what we create. We understand that intuitively in the case of heterosexual persons. We not only allow, and honor, but in everlasting ways we celebrate commitment between heterosexual persons. Not only weddings, but the wedding anniversaries of heterosexual couples have created a virtual industry. Meanwhile, many of those persons who celebrate their own marriages, and those of their parents and children, strenuously oppose marriage for homosexual couples. None the less, the effect of gay liberation overall has not been in the direction of greater promiscuity but tends toward more committed relationships. That is observable over the last twenty or so years. Mature gay men, and women, want the rewards of lasting companionship, fidelity, and family. Matchmaking agencies for gays, abound as they do for non-gays.

A tougher question is one regarding those who never marry, because their commitment is not acknowledged, or perhaps because they never have that opportunity. Should they endeavor to live their lives as though they were nonsexual beings, though that is not a choice they have? Should intimacy be altogether restricted to those fortunate enough or who choose to be married? Can some persons have warm, caring, reciprocal sexual intimacy that makes them better, more whole, functional, and caring persons than the unbearable burden of lifelong abstinence? Some heterosexual widowed persons do just that for a variety of reasons. Sometimes those reasons have to do with finances or with family relationships.

As persons must work to perfect their minds, bodies, and spirits, so the perfecting of one's sexuality is a journey, and one related to those other journeys of mind, body, and spirit. There are far more ways to get it wrong than to get it right. The road is a straight and narrow one in that there are boundaries inherent to love and truth. But the road, the way, is not so straight nor narrow that a mere mortal cannot travel upon it.

Life is a journey and we are not always on the right road. But that is true of almost everything about our lives. It is true for heterosexual as well as homosexual persons. Perhaps it is what is meant by *"we are all sinners."* We all begin in imperfection, or incompleteness, and our lives are journeys toward realizing our right and full humanity. This is not a *"good works"* theology, because our journeys are not ones to earn God's love but to realize and actualize that very unconditional love in our lives.

Chapter 8

The Vanishing Jesus - or "The Uncarnation"

> *"Among those who went up to worship at the festival were some Greeks. They came to Philip, who was from Bethsaida in Galilee, and said to him, 'Sir, we wish to see Jesus.' "*
>
> John 12:20-21

This verse from John has often been the text for an evangelistic message. The thrust of such a sermon has usually been to proclaim the resurrected Christ rather than the not-yet-crucified Jesus. But as the crucifixion had not yet happened, and they did know it would happen, it was Jesus, the man, they were asking to see. It was only the man who could bring credibility to the claims of divinity.

Several years ago I began to notice that among many Christians, Jesus - not the suffering Jesus on the cross, not the miracle working Jesus - but Jesus, the man, the teacher, was disappearing, etherealized into the religious mist. Even so, the dying one on the cross was still there, his precious and miraculous blood extolled as the only means of salvation. Though the Gospels are often quoted, they seem edited; much that Jesus said and did is being left out, ignored, or changed.

For some, his death seems in fact to be theologically convenient in that he no longer has to be looked upon as in any real sense - human. The man who was born as all others are born, even though many believe he was conceived differently, seems less and less spoken of among many of his followers. The man who was an infant before he was a youth and a youth before he was man is vanishing. What has been disappearing is the man of the villages around the Sea of Galilee, the mixer who spent time with those who were thought disreputable by the very religious, the man who conversed with women as though they were as significant as men, the man who set his face toward Jerusalem, the man of personal encounters, the man of passions, the itinerant preacher, the teacher. This man has among many been vanishing. On film it's called a "dissolve," and where one image fades, another appears. Exit Jesus, enter Jehovah.

Have I been imagining this? I turn on my car radio to various broadcasts of fundamentalist preachers - not hard to find. On my car radio there doesn't seem to be any other kind. This raises the question, why not? There is much quoting of Paul, and of Genesis and Leviticus, and many references to apocalyptic literature. Whole sermons are sometimes constructed from a dependent clause in a single verse. But Jesus, the friend, the comforter and counselor, the teacher, the man who was very much on earth before he was in heaven, seems to have ascended, no footprint remaining of the real man who had walked on earth, no fingerprints, no DNA. It is as though he had been one who walked without leaving footprints. The incarnation was being turned into the uncarnation.

The Church had often had trouble with Jesus, the man, the mixer, the person of flesh. Certainly for the first three centuries of the "Christian Era," it struggled with the paradox of his divine/human natures, formally resolving the issue in the Council of Nicea in 325 A.D. *"For us and for our salvation he came down from heaven, was incarnate of the Holy Spirit and the virgin Mary and became truly human."* (The Nicene Creed) Though many fear that the divinity of Jesus will be denied, it is far more likely that it is his humanity that will be denied, even if lip service is given to it. The difficulty in accepting Jesus' humanity never, of course, went away all together; believing that God truly became man is not only beyond human comprehension, but to many may also seem somehow lacking in true devotion, especially if one can only conceive of flesh as evil.

Probably nothing is more difficult for persons to accept in the humanity of Jesus than the reality that if fully human he was, therefore, a sexual being. Though we don't talk or think about him that way, we should reflect on what it means that he was sexual. Did Jesus experience sexual attraction, even passion? I do not ask the question lightly, and certainly not for effect, but because we should ask ourselves why such questions, or conjecture, is disturbing. If we can say he was at the beginning, and through him were all things made that were made, including our sexuality (part of what the creator declared to be "good"), and yet it is an unthinkable and repugnant thought to us that Jesus truly was a sexual being, with sexual feelings, then we need to ask ourselves what our reaction means. If we really cannot fathom that, then we really do not accept him as being fully human. A person's sexuality is not an extraneous, detachable, or dispensable aspect of his or her humanity. Neither was it expendable to Jesus' humanity.

I have become aware recently of a sharp increase in the marketing of angels and things angel related. Angels have appeared - and appeared - and appeared - in every gift shop and book store. The gender of angels, if they have gender, has been confusing. In the Bible they are all depicted as male - Michael and Gabriel, etc.; in gift shops, and greenhouse nurseries where they are sold as lawn and garden statuary, they are almost always female. Perhaps in our culture being an angel seems more a feminine than a masculine role. Only a grinch would object to angels. Angels are marketable in a way that Jesus, as human, is not. And it's not surprising. There is a lot about Jesus that is not nearly so comforting as your very own guardian angel.

++++

I have a friend, a gay man, who lives in Vera Cruz, New Mexico. Every year he, and usually his partner, travel at their own expense to wherever the General Assembly of our Church is meeting. *(Since I wrote this Presbyterian General Assemblies have become biannual.) Their purpose is simply to stand for hours each day outside the Assembly Hall, or where commissioners are going back and forth to meetings, to hold signs about welcoming gay and lesbian persons into the Church. David has a big, warm, happy, bearded face. (Put him in a red suit and you have Santa Claus - nothing need be added.) He simply stands there in silent witness, though persons come up to him from time to time to comment, usually favorably, about his sign. Sometimes the comments are negative. On the last day of the Assembly several years ago he was holding a sign saying, accurately, that Jesus never said a single word about same sex relationships. One man paused several feet away to look for a few moments at this sign and then came over and said, *"Well, he should have."* There are those who would like to correct what Jesus did, or fill in what they believe he left out. It makes me think of something from *"The Brothers Karamazov."*

In that novel by Dostoyevsky I was remembering, *"The Legend of the Grand Inquisitor."* When I was in my twenties this famous passage had a profound impact on my struggle to find what was for me a credible theology. This legend tells of a fantasy that one of the brothers, Ivan, has made up and relates to his saintly brother, Alyosha, a monk. In this legend, Jesus silently appears in Seville at the height of the Spanish inquisition. The Grand Inquisitor intuitively knows that the silent man is Jesus and has him arrested and put in prison. At night, the Inquisitor comes to him there. In what is surely one of the greatest passages of modern literature, the Grand Inquisitor tells the silent Christ that they, the Church, have "corrected" what he, Jesus, has done in giving man an unbearable freedom. In compassion they, the Church, have taken that freedom from the people and mercifully told them what to believe and what to do, and they are happy and beholden because the Church alone mediates forgiveness to them.

It told a truth that I perhaps had already discovered but could not have articulated. We use our religion to reinvent Jesus the way we want him to be - and then silence him - lest our manipulations of the Gospels become too evident. The vanishing Jesus I am talking about has by many been put out of sight and silenced lest who he is, and what he said and did, would destroy the religion others have invented in his name. Neal expressed it well:

There's a great line in 'Inherit the Wind' about the Scopes trial. The two lawyers (Clarence Darrow and William Jennings Bryant) are talking to each other and Darrow says, "God created man in his own image and man being the gentleman that he is has returned the favor." If we talk about God as "Father" and "Son," all these words are human symbols and ideas we have projected onto God to try and understand and put labels to some of the revelations....we tend to animate God with these human attributes...and we think our motives are pure and well intentioned. Therefore, if we feel like smacking someone because we're angry, then God must be angry at them too because they're bad people. And my understanding now about all our misery and suffering isn't that it is from God; it's what we do to each other.
Neal

Part of creating God in our own image has been to create God as one who hates what we hate and loves what we love. For many that includes hating what they perceive as the "sin" of homosexuality.

In the prologue of the Gospel of John the author speaks of The Word coming into the world "...*full of grace and truth.*" In Jesus, then, what do we see? Who do we see? Any honest look will observe a man who associated with the sick and dying, the poor, lepers, the lame, the blind, the deaf, demoniacs (we would call mentally ill), Gentiles, Romans (including a Centurion, and the Centurion's servant whom he healed), Samaritans, prisoners, tax collectors, winebibbers and sinners, and children. He associated with some who were rich and powerful; such as the rich young ruler (who may have been more than just a figure in a parable), Joseph of Aramathia, and Nicodemus. And he also associated with women in ways unprecedented among those of his religion, culture, and gender. The women included those thought to be of "loose character" (the woman caught in adultery, the woman at the well); ardent, passionate women like Mary of Bethany and Mary Magdalene (who was perhaps the woman who washed his feet with costly ointment); and persistent women; the one with the flow of blood (Matthew 9:20), and the Syrophonecian woman (Mark 7:26).

He was a teacher whose words, especially in parables, expressed God's passionate reaching out to embrace the lost and the hurting; and to commend those who serve them. The parables of the lost sheep, the lost coin, the good Samaritan, and especially the story of the prodigal son, reveal a God who reaches out to embrace those most dispossessed or discarded by others. In Jesus, we have one who in his major discourses identified himself with the poor, the outcast, the marginalized, and those the English writer Colin Wilson identified as *"The Outsider."* In the beatitudes of the Sermon on tbe Mount, in his sermon in the synagogue in Nazareth, and in his message about separating the sheep and the goats in *Matthew 25*, he identifies himself with the those who are least in the eyes of others. He is a person who passionately opposes the oppressors and exploiters of these persons; the Scribes and Pharisees, the legalists, the money changers, and the sanctimonious. He even criticized the criticizers, those of his own company who judged each other, Martha when she criticizes Mary, Judas when he criticizes the woman with the ointment.

Looking at the Gospels as a whole, there is nothing more conspicuous than that those who wrote them intended to convey that the Jesus they witnessed, confessed and followed was a man who related with ardent, tireless, uncompromising compassion and sympathy to every sort of social outcast, to the outsider, to those Simon and Garfunkel called the "*sat upon, the spat upon, the ratted on...*" (Sounds of Silence). On the other hand, he was passionately critical of those who exercised the arrogance of power, the exploiters, the self-righteous, the conspicuously pious, and the judgmental. He was unintimidated by the powerful, and unabashedly associated with those of "*low estate*." He sided with the oppressed and confronted their oppressors.

The image of the Jesus of the Gospels has been polished by the Church to a veritable gloss. But beneath that is still the rough stone. It is absolutely astonishing to see how the Gospels have been totally flip-flopped by some who profess his name, so that Jesus is made to seem the teacher and endorser of virtually everything he hated and opposed.

Another aspect of the vanishing Jesus has been the tendency to take some of the sensuality out of the gospels, turning, as it were, succulent fruit to dried fruit, turning plums to prunes and grapes to raisins. Though the Gospels were written many years after Jesus' death, those who wrote them put great importance on touching, touching that is remembered. Our bodies and not just our minds have memory. We know that being touched in wrong ways can leave horrific memories, but being touched in good ways has a powerful, lasting, and healing effect.

The centerpiece of the Church's life through history has been something sensual, something related to the senses: the Lord's Supper. We have tended to turn that succulent fruit to dried fruit. Rather than it being a feast of abundance, it has often been minimized with tiny cubes of bread and thimble sized glasses of grape juice served, in some Protestant Churches, as infrequently as Church law will permit. There is often no sense of abundance. It has been intellectualized and made, though inadvertently, as stark as possible. And maybe we should give the Baptists credit that baptism by immersion - which lacks neatness - preserves more the sensuality of the Gospels. Many mainline Protestants, somewhat compulsive about order, have minimized that one, as well. I suspect that immersion carries a stronger memory than the "baptism lite" of my own tradition. David remembers his:

Our church was really small, and we always baptized our members in the river. Well, it had rained the day before and the river had risen and the current was swift. At first, there was some discussion about not doing the service, but then they decided to go through with it. I guess because we were Christians we thought we were invincible. So anyway, we got down there and the current was really strong and I remember thinking as I was wading out to the minister, "What if they lose me? What if I'm swept away? What if as I'm drowning I panic and accidentally swear or take the Lord's name in vain? Will I go to hell?"

The vanishing Jesus is the one who cursed the fig tree because it bore no fruit, the one who provided the finest wine at Cana in great abundance, a richer more celebrative wine, the one who broke the bread to the men on the Emmaus Road evoking their memory of the one who had perhaps often broken bread to them, and the one who provided the abundant loaves and fishes (We emphasize the miracle if that is what it was, but the Gospel emphasizes the abundance.) This vanishing Jesus suffered the accusation of his being a winebibber and sinner. Contrasting himself with the austerity of John the Baptist He says:

How can I describe this generation? They are like children sitting in the market-place and shouting at each other, "We piped for you and you would not dance. We wept and wailed, and you would not mourn," For John came, neither eating nor drinking, and they say, "He is possessed." The Son of Man came eating and drinking, and they say, "Look at him, a glutton and drinker, a friend of tax-gatherers and sinners!"

(Matthew 11:16-19).

It is this man, this strange, uncompromising, passionate, and sometimes solitary man, this sexual man, of gendered body but universal soul, this man born in a stable and executed on a cross, who is our Sovereign and Savior - and our friend. And He is the friend of gays as truly and as deeply as the friend of any others, though they have often been torn between Jesus as friend and brother - and God as the tyrannical father. Many gays have had to escape the voices and attitudes of those who seem to feel they are in charge of making up God's guest list - which does not include self-affirming homosexuals. Jesus, thankfully, is allowed to choose His own friends rather than have them chosen for Him.

Allen sums it up:

I see Jesus as a personal friend, and certainly I see Jesus as a man. I guess that's all I need to say about it. To me Jesus is a very personal close friend.

++++

One of the ironies of fundamentalism is that for all its Jesus talk, many of its adherents pay little more than lip service to the Jesus of the Gospels. Their true focus is not on grace but law. Law is at the center of what very often is an ancestral, tribal, patriarchal religion.

I was in Montana a few years ago to officiate at the wedding of a nephew. Having performed wedding ceremonies in several states other than the one in which I reside, I assumed (as is required in most states) that I would need before the wedding to go to the local courthouse and register in some way (showing some sort of professional credential) to make my signature on the license valid. Surprisingly, it turned out that in Montana nothing is required. The Clerk explained it simply, "*In Montana anyone can marry anyone*." The point of this, however, has nothing to do with weddings only about the occasion of my going to the courthouse.

As I entered this large stone 1920's structure that stands commandingly at the head of Main Street in the town where I grew up, I saw that something had been added since my youth. A stone tablet had been erected by her front door inscribed with the ten commandments. I thought it was interesting that the townsfolk had chosen to raise a tablet not with the great commandment on it, found in the New as well as the Old Testament, but one with the ten commandments. The courthouse had been, in my youth, the place where trials took place, and immediately behind it was the county jail. (Progress has come to our town and new courtrooms are now in a modern adjacent building.) The erection of this stone tablet at the head of Main Street, in what was designed to be the focal point of this town, has to do with law, and as a rod for the straightening of youth. Perhaps our religion is, after all, more commonly about law than about the values and relationships that underlie and interpret the law, which is contained in the great commandment "...*to love the Lord your God with all your heart, and mind, and soul, and strength...and your neighbor as yourself.*"

Why, then, all the Jesus talk? Because many want to claim that Jesus is the endorser of their perverted faith. Truth is that the distortion is usually rooted in self-deception. Persons believe what they are saying. To a large degree it has come down to them on the floorboards of their village church, the flannelgraph stories in Sunday School, the raucous but repetitious gospel hymns, and beneath the revival tent.

I remember thinking I was not as afraid of Jesus as I was of God. Jesus seemed like a much nicer guy and much less likely to smote me if I did something wrong. I remember when I was really small, and my father was still preaching, there was no childrens' church and all us kids were just expected to sit through this long dull service. We were allowed to draw pictures as long as they had something to do with church. Well, I always drew pictures of the rapture. Jesus up in the sky, and all us Christians flying up to meet him. It was great! All the sinners are on the ground, presumably dead I guess. I remember at that age that thinking of Jesus always made me feel safe.

I saw those pictures again a few years ago - my mother saves everything - and I noticed that in most of the pictures, right there next to Jesus, I had also drawn Russian bombs falling from the sky. This was the early sixties and our church was a designated fallout shelter. We had one of those yellow and black signs on the outside of the building. But I don't remember ever feeling the least scared because Jesus was our savior and the sooner the Russians dropped those bombs the better. That just meant we'd get to heaven sooner.

But then I turned thirteen and all that changed. At thirteen you were expected to go forward during the altar call and publicly declare that you were a Christian. Well, I managed to delay that until I was fifteen, but I remember those altar calls Sunday after Sunday. I always dreaded them. The organist would play, "Softly and Tenderly, Jesus is calling," over and over, while the minister kept saying,"Come on down. Tomorrow may be too late. You could be in a car accident on your way home today and you could be lost forever." And there was this awful guilt about the whole thing. You were reminded of all that Christ had done for you and how horribly he suffered. "Won't you come on down? Is it so little to ask that you come - now?" All of a sudden Jesus seemed like such an injured, broken person. Guilt soaked I didn't want to look at him. I wanted to turn my eyes away.

It's so different now. I was raised with this idea of Jesus as this supernatural person who could fly and read your mind and walk through walls. Now, when I think of him, I tend to think of him as a man, but an extraordinary man, an extraordinary teacher.

David

I attended a conference in Atlanta where the welcoming address was given by a local pastor. He sought to explain to those gathered, who were engaged in ministries to and with gays and lesbians, the cultural conservatism often found in southern churches. His perspective on that was that many southerners had stepped outside and had seen a conspicuously unjust society that they had helped create and preserve, and they stepped back inside the church and put their faith in a religion of personal salvation - not of social change. Such religion is far more likely to emphasize the divinity than the humanity of Jesus.

Early in my ministry I served a church in northern Virginia at a time when there was a struggle to end segregation in our churches. Those opposed to this change in the Church argued that, "*politics and religion don't mix.*" That argument seemed to be abandoned when Jerry Falwell decided to mix them. "*You can't legislate morality,*" they said, until Pat Robertson convinced many that morality could be, and should be, legislated. Segregation is particularly indefensible if one takes seriously the humanity of Jesus, who identified himself with those oppressed.

"What We Evangelicals Believe," was a book that seemed as though it would be a fairly authoritative source of what evangelicals believe about Jesus. The book by David Allen Hubbard, former President of Fuller Seminary, is a brief exposition of the articles of that seminary's "statement of faith." I could find only a few sentences on Jesus as man and those emphasized the miraculous: the virgin birth, the resurrection; and his perfect life. Of the incarnation Hubbard writes:

A marvelous display of spiritual information? Yes, and much more. A tantalizing exhibit of miraculous power? Yes, and other things. A compelling curriculum of ethical instruction, of course. But that is not all. A tragic story which has provided a human catharsis so that we can handle further tragedy? No doubt, for some. But above all Jesus Christ is the fulfillment, the culmination of God's unbending drive to make himself known as Savior...the invisible God made himself fleshly to all who would truly see and hear.

"Fleshly?" Somehow that doesn't sound like real flesh but something like flesh, a simulation of flesh. It makes me want to find him, not in bleached robes, but as a man of real flesh among those, winebibbers and sinners though they may be, who cope daily with the realities of being flesh and blood.

The emphasis on Jesus among many evangelicals and fundamentalists is almost exclusively on his birth (...*of a virgin, angels, wise men, etc. - the miraculous*) and his death *(blood sacrifice to atone for sins and appease God's wrath, the bodily resurrection, the ascension, etc. - again the miraculous)*. What lies in between those two events in Jesus' life, except where miracle is involved, is of little interest to them. Whatever cannot be put into the service of evangelism and "conversion" fails to attract their attention, and that means whatever does not generate fear and guilt is not that useful.

I've heard preachers trying to make the point that Jesus really was a "man's man." They place great emphasis on his being a carpenter and the muscle they believe that would require; or they talk about his driving the money changers out of the Temple, or how strong he must have been to bear the cross (though he fell beneath it and it was put on the shoulders of Simon of Cyrene, and the soldiers were surprised at how quickly he died). What's all this about, I wondered? Why this need to establish his masculinity? They can talk about the cross or the miracles but the one-on-one stories and Jesus' teachings are problematic for them. Perhaps they feel in these passages a "feminine side" - a soft side - in Jesus that makes them uncomfortable. Maybe they have an inward fear that Jesus is not a "guy's guy," not "a man's man," after all. Maybe they fear Jesus is a sissy, soft on sin, a "bleeding heart." Well, in the most literal way possible he is indeed a bleeding heart. Lucky for us that he is. That last statement is not, by the way, a plug for "substitutionary atonement." By his stripes we are healed - yes - but not by some kind of magic, but because his stripes are the inevitable outcome and outpouring of his love.

Bottom line? Jesus, as person, is not their kind of "guy," not their cup of tea - nor mug of beer. The incarnation, except as it serves their doctrine of substitutionary atonement, of appeasing God's eternal wrath, is of little interest to them. They call God father, but he is a terrible and terrifying father. I am a father. I would never expect my child, or anyone's child, to be in every way perfect, as no one is, if we could even define "perfect." But I have never felt wrath toward my child, or that my dignity was unbearably offended by any imperfection there might be in him. (I am more inclined to be aware of my own imperfections than his.) I never felt that sacrifice was necessary for him to appease my righteous anger. How would such an attitude go along with being a loving father - or mother? Grace with some of these is less than amazing. It barely takes the edge off God's wrathful judgment.

The inevitable outcome of what Jesus said and what he did was for him to be arrested, tortured, tried, and publicly executed. The trial was a mockery of justice, the execution a lynching. We've fancied up the cross in a million ways, hung it around our necks and dangled it from our ears. We've encrusted it with jewels, festooned it with flowers, embroidered it on silk and fine linen. We've carved it from exotic woods, from stone, and marble, and cast it in precious metals. Some have even tattooed it on their bodies. But for the one nailed to the cross, it was a crude and sadistic instrument of execution, as it was intended to be by those who put him there.

If Jesus had been executed by hanging, would we wear a diamond studded noose around our necks, or fashion one of rosewood and center it on our chancel wall? Would we render it in stained glass, and place a lighted one atop our steeple? Perhaps we would. But, just as we can almost no longer recognize the cross for what it was, so we can scarcely recognize the man who hung there and why he was there.

Love is not an attribute in the realm of God, it is the essence of it, its ordering principle, and its manifestation. Love is the goal of the Gospel. To love is the essence of maturity - of coming of age - to love God with all your heart and mind and soul and strength. We have seen God acting through the infancy of the Church and, more recently, through her adolescence. We are still there, stumbling toward maturity, struggling to grow up and be adult. Who is our model for what it means to be an adult? Jesus is the model of adulthood, of real maturity. Jesus is the one truly mature person, the one who loves us perfectly, and the one who enables us to love others.

Much of the Church has been fading on Jesus, the man, fearing perhaps the countenance they will see. To bring him sharply into focus will, at last, bring our gay brothers and sisters into focus as well. For those who would see Jesus they may discover that He is to be found in the company of those they feel are unworthy.

Chapter 9

The Disoriented Male

> *"I cry at movies, I cry at plays. I guess I'm just very tenderhearted when it comes to some situations. Yet on the other hand, I think it is a good attribute. Maybe it's gay, maybe it's not; but I think it's O.K. to cry and I think men should do more of it."*
>
> Allen

Many men born in the first half of the twentieth century - white, heterosexual men - have experienced a gradual, sustained, if somewhat convulsive, dismantling of their white, male, heterosexual privilege. The civil rights movement was the first great assault asserting that Caucasians were not a chosen people, a superior race, and not entitled to special privilege, nor closed community,

The second great assault, which felt like betrayal, came from wives and daughters, even mothers, some of whom refused, even symbolically, to be treated as the property of men. These women redefined their roles, and reimagined themselves - without male consent.

As women began to find their identity, many men began to lose theirs, and no one was paying much attention to that. Men don't cry, right? Men can take care of themselves. How were they to express their pain, their dislocation? The old patriarch began just to look like an old fool, like Archie Bunker. Well, not quite like Archie because Norman Lear let us laugh at Archie but only through laughter with love in it. Lear somehow always made Archie appealing even when appalling. Perhaps it was because we always perceived that in Archie, underneath, was the child bucking up to be a man in his father's eyes.

The third great assault has been on male sexuality. It began to be asserted by gays that homosexuality is not inferior to heterosexuality, and that those of differing sexual orientation should be entitled to equality. This was perhaps the deepest assault of all for those to whom it seemed their sexuality was what most defined them as men. And in a way, even more deeply than with women's liberation, it felt like a betrayal, this time coming from their own gender.

If you have a patriarchal culture where men are on top, a threat to that culture deep down is very scary not only to men but to some women as well. To think you're to lose some privilege or power, it is a scary thing. And losing it to females is one thing, but to lose it to males that you perceive to act like females, who are in essence forfeiting their rights as heterosexual males who exercise dominion and control over God's creation, to actually, willfully, give that up, you are a traitor. It's the fear of losing power, and the women's groups are trying to take it away, and they are over half the population. And now, we've got some of our own trying to take it away, too. It's a frightening thing, and I think that's where some of the backlash and the homophobia and the violence and that sort of stuff comes from. They perceive us as being traitors to their gender and privilege.

Neal

What is the meaning of the religious right's fanaticism about gun possession? Gun possession for many men is a mark of their masculinity. The fear (though unfounded) that their guns might be taken away seems to them to be a threat to take away their manhood, an emasculating act by a sissy government. They are imprinted with this mark of masculinity almost from birth.

One of the first "toys" put in many boys hands is some version of a gun. To many it seems that - more than blue booties - this is in part how he will know he is a boy and not a girl.

One very deft commentary on this current state of the male has been in the movie, and now the stage musical, "The Full Monty." Here working men in a blue collar community (In the movie, Sheffield, England, and in the stage musical, Buffalo, New York) are recently laid off from their jobs in a steel company. They are in various stages of trying to cope not only with their financial problems but with the shame of applying for unemployment or being urged by family to go get a minimum wage job at Wal-Mart.

Traditional males, they feel impotent and paralyzed in their failure to fulfill their masculine role, having become breadwinners who aren't bringing home the bread. Two of them pull a former co-worker from his car in which he is attempting to asphyxiate himself. They feel acutely the loss of esteem from their wives and families. The central character is faced with the threat of losing custody of his twelve year old son because of lapsed child support. One man, the other men's former supervisor, has been desperately engaged in keeping his laid-off status a secret from his wife while she, unknowing, is running up bills on their credit card. The wolf is at the door. Another, who is overweight, has such low self-esteem he can't make love to his wife.

This movie and musical finds its comedic power in the triumph of these men when "for one night only" they perform as male strippers - going for the full Monty (the completely naked male). These are not Chippendale dancers. They are neither particularly handsome nor buff, nor are they dancers. They are just a variety of ordinary men, and that is the precise power of this timely metaphor of the disoriented male, American or otherwise. Their triumph comes at several levels: in attracting a crowd of women, including their appreciative wives, and making enough money in their single performance to restore their dignity. But most of all their triumph comes, symbolically, in revealing their unemasculated selves.

Throughout human history, in most cultures, life has been structured around male supremacy. Only in the late 20th Century did that begin to change, and the change has been disorienting for men. A great many men are wounded and in crisis, especially those who had stern, domineering, and sometimes abusive fathers. As women's roles have changed, the power they have gained has been felt by many men as a loss of power - and identity. At the same time many liberated women send a confusing message. They still want a man to be a man in the old stereotypical way. The male has to walk that line between a woman's new sense of autonomy and freedom and her desire to be pursued, courted, romanced, and cared for in the old way.

Having officiated at a great many weddings, which involves, in each case, several hours of counseling the about-to-be-married, I'm aware that it is usually far more the bride's day than the groom's, whose role is primarily to show up. And often what the bride wants, and usually the groom, and the parents of both, and the guests who arrive - is "tradition." Underlying that tradition is the solemnization of a contractual arrangement whereby a father, not a father and mother, but a father "gives away" his daughter who promises to "love, honor, and obey" her husband, take his name, and bear *his* children. A cautionary question used to be a standard part of the service, and in many services may still be included, "*If anyone has reason why these two should not be joined in holy matrimony, speak now or forever hold your peace.*" This was in case there were any legal objections to its going forward (possibly that the groom already has a wife somewhere, or the bride is being passed off as new merchandise when in fact she is "damaged goods.") That question hopefully has been dropped from most marriage ceremonies, but that has only been in recent years.

To be fair, for most couples these traditions have taken on a patina of romantic feeling, and are not to be taken literally by the participants or the witnesses. I don't know how it may be in other churches, even other churches of my own denomination, but today in those I am familiar with the "love, honor, and obey" has usually been replaced by more mutual, egalitarian, vows. When I am officiating I do not ask, "Who gives this woman to be married to this man?" but "Who presents this man and woman to be married?", (the same would apply if it were two men or two women being married) and fathers and mothers on both sides respond. Many women retain their maiden name coupling it with their husband's, often using it without their husband's name in their professional role. And it is expected that if they have children, they are the trust of both and the property of neither. Times have changed but some attitudes linger.

Several years ago counseling a couple at whose wedding I would be officiating, I asked them, as I usually do in premarital counseling, how they envisioned their future life together. I want to be sure that those about to be married have shared with each other their expectations of the future in case they should discover that they are on divergent paths and possibly motivated by very different values. That is not usually the case, but the purpose of the exercise is to discover if deep differences do exist so that they at least communicate with each other about those differences before they marry.

The couple I was meeting with were both young professional persons. She answered first saying that she thought she would probably continue to work for several years and that then she might want to retire. She saw herself as "liberated" and assumed this meant she should have choices. I asked her if she believed her husband should also have similar choices as to his work life. The question actually seemed to stun her. Though she assumed her liberation meant having choices, she made no such assumption about her intended husband, and he didn't either; he pretty much assumed his role was fixed.

Women's roles have been reexamined but, by and large, men's roles have not. Many men feel disempowered, and rather than seek a deliberate kind of reorientation - which itself is somewhat contrary to their conditioning as males, they may be reactive, becoming aggressive, or dropping out. This leads to a lot of disintegration of family. The fundamentalist's solution for that is for everyone to return to their old masculine/feminine roles. Therefore, you get things like "Promisekeepers," and other male bonding fraternities.

Though most men obviously are not gay, many require some kind of "cover" for their affections toward other men so that their masculinity is not called into question. The military provides that. The real reason for "don't ask, don't tell" may have been that if gays could serve openly in the military, then being a soldier and being straight would not be as synonymous as they have been presumed to be. Policemen and firemen often experience a bond not offered in most other male dominated professions because of the possibility that in some circumstances their lives may be in each other's hands.

Many team sports like football, hockey, baseball, and basketball, strong on physical contact, not only offer men the opportunity for exhibiting aggression, but also an opportunity for releasing emotions in the company of other men. Few of these persons, of course, are gay (it would be too great a generalization to say none - ever), but "straight" men often feel great risk in allowing their emotions to be visible, especially any that are directed toward other men.

Less so today, but in the past that risk was often felt even in the relationship between fathers and sons.

Sports - team sports, combative sports, sports that simulate war, and the watching of these combats with other men, rooting for one side to win, placing bets with your co-workers - are rites, as almost everyone knows, of masculine identity. Newscasters often transition over to the weatherman (if it is a man) with some sort of "guy" comment about last night's game. The weatherman had better have seen or read about last night's game and be ready with a little repartee or he is going to look like he didn't eat his Wheaties.

These little rituals are so commonplace in our society that they go by without notice to almost everyone except someone who doesn't know or care who played, let alone who won, last night's game. In sports men can slap each others butts, and in victory they may not only "high five," but leap into each others arms, and there is no threat to their masculinity because it is all in a masculine context.

Combat is in the movies they watch, and the video games they play. It comes under the category of "fun," but is often deadly serious. Similar combat is often carried over into politics and religion. In religion some fundamentalists call it spiritual warfare. It is of great importance to win, to triumph over one's enemies, even in matters of the Spirit. Fundamentalists love the word "victory." "*Victory in Jesus!*" they sing.

It would be far too great a generalization to say that gay men are not interested in watching and participating in contact sports, and unfortunately that idea is part of the stereotype of gay men. It may be true that many are more attracted to sports such as swimming, tennis, skating, or gymnastics, where one's victories are more often in the achievement of a personal best. They may be more inclined to compete against themselves than others, or to seek a payoff in cooperation rather than combat.

The drive to win over others, harping back to perhaps some primordial instinct, is often less present in gay men. They have already, so to speak, lost or forfeited the battle for traditional male identify, therefore, they have a certain freedom to define themselves apart from the old stereotype. This exhilarating freedom is perhaps part of what puts the "gaiety" in gay.

In the Church, and somewhat in society at large, the struggle between gays and those opposed to their ordination, is an oddly pitched battle. It is very often a conflict between the meek and the militant, between those who want justice but do not want to be aggressive, and those who feel that they must "go to war" so that the infidels (gays) do not win. The more that change seems inevitable the more militant they become.

It might be said that it is also an oddly pitched battle in that it is often one between the "humorful" and "humorless." Gays, out of some necessity, often are well practiced in using humor in self defense, but those on the other side, especially those who are "religious," tend to associate such humor with decadence and are not amused.

It is garden variety paranoia which probably accounts for most fundamentalist's treatment of homosexuals. They may fear something in the homosexual that they subconsciously fear in themselves. That does not mean that they are homosexual, only that we are not as differentiated in our sexual feelings as we think - or hope - we are. Men can feel affection for other men under the cover of their masculine image; but an openly homosexual person is threatening because his affection for another man may have a sexual component. In a better world men could feel affection for other men without the need for cover. And there are now many heterosexual men who can do that. There has even been a new word coined for them, metrosexuals. Deep friendship between heterosexual and homosexual men is explored in two significant films "Big Eden," and the Cuban film, "Strawberries and Chocolate."

Many of the younger generation, having come into a world where change has already happened, experience these greater, if yet imperfect, equalities as normal and positive, including gay liberation.

One of the things I find most surprising - and I'm very grateful for - is that I can go out to lunch with a gay male friend and we can sit there and talk about our relationships, who we're dating, and how it's going, and just totally commiserate. I can go out the next day with a female friend and talk about her relationships and feel like I totally understand her point of view. And then I can go out with a straight male friend and talk about his relationships and feel like I totally relate to his situation as well. It's one of the mysteries of being gay. You straddle these different worlds. I have this feminine side to me, this masculine side to me, and then there is this other in between self that I guess is my gay self. I find it interesting to feel I'm a citizen of many countries in a strange kind of way, and that I speak many languages. I have a lot of straight male friends and I'm really proud of most of these guys, especially when they ask me who I'm dating. It's always a little awkward but I find it kind of courageous of them. I know on some level they'll never understand that part of my life, but they, at least, make the effort. It means a lot to me. I know it can't be easy for them.

David

Having become aware several years ago of a pattern in male/female relationships as depicted in popular literature, cartoons, films, and sitcoms, I was amazed at how often it appears in various aspects of popular culture. This cartoon of the male, though unflattering in many ways, is one which both men and women seem to enjoy. It is the "boys will be boys" version of the lives of men. It is the premise of many situation comedies and hundreds of commercials. This situation is for example the premise of much of the comedy in "Everyone Loves Raymond." The husband, Ray Romano, is a constantly bumbling inarticulate husband, always in the doghouse with his wife who seems to be a far more sophisticated and complex creature who with a mixture of love and long suffering regards him not so much as a man as a boy.

The characters in "The King of Queens," "How I Met Your Mother," and "Rules of Engagement" partake of the same formula for comedy. Though it was more complex, Archie and Edith Bunker were another variation on this theme. Edith treated Archie as a boy and forgave him much. The English TV sitcom "Keeping Up Appearances," utilizes the theme in a very broad, over-the-top comic style. Even Lucy Ricardo and Desi, and certainly Fred and Ethel Mertz follow the model, as did Gleason in "The Honeymooners." Charlie Brown and Lucy are the very archetype of this. There were "The Flintstones," "Dagwood and Blondie" (Dagwood Bumstead - that name says it all). Then there is Tarzan (the apeman) and Jane, who civilizes him. Even Clark Kent and Lois Lane follow this pattern, except that Clark has a secret life as a superhuman hero (is that male fantasy?). One might even detect this pattern in the story of Adam and Eve.

This pattern presents men either as a simpler life form, more one dimensional than women, or the straight man for a ditsy wife, i.e. Lucy, or Hyacinth Bucket in "Keeping Up Appearances. " One has it not only in many sitcoms, but it is a common theme in commercials - perhaps the most common theme. Women have lives. Many men are, in their basic state, barely evolved from the caveman. Men are often depicted as couch potatoes and slobs addicted to sitting in front of the TV watching sports. The only thing the couch potato might be more interested in than sports is sex, for which in many of these sitcoms he often has to barter and beg. Girls grow up and become women, but boys simply grow up to be boys, howbeit sometimes lovable ones. As you watch TV commercials, and programs, observe how often you see that. In all of this the woman is the actor, the man, the acted upon.

Perhaps women are more complex because for them life, under patriarchy, has required that. Under patriarchy the male is the head of the family, but the woman is often the real power behind the throne - the throne sometimes being a ratty recliner parked in front of a TV. Her power has often been in the past more covert than overt; that is a more complex role. The male, who might be quite sophisticated and capable in other aspects of his life (Ray Romano as a sports writer, is sometimes alluded to but almost never seen), seems almost a dumb animal, Neanderthal, in his domestic environment. Freud's question, "What do women want?" seems to be the daily conundrum of these men's lives.

A paradoxical feature of male/female relationships is that those cultures we often think of as being patriarchal - African-American, Hispanic, Jewish, Southern European, etc. - are usually at the same time strongly matriarchal. Though patriarchal in their formal structure they are at the same time matriarchal in style. Out of these often comes the "macho syndrome," a somewhat instinctive male assertion of power.

Underlying much of the culture of patriarchy is an implicit expectation that men will manifest their "superiority" and "right to dominate" by distinguishing themselves from the "weaknesses" and "vulnerabilities" of women. This means being more tightly reigned in emotionally than women except in contexts, like battle, that exhibit their strength, bravery, and devotion. It is problematic for some men that women in the military, especially if in a battle situation, demonstrate that such qualities are by no means exclusively male.

There was an article in U.S. News and World Report with a picture of a boy on the cover, that says, "The Weaker Sex." Inside, it says that men are actually more emotional than women. Studies now show that men try to hide it which creates greater stress on their bodies...very interesting.
John

That's why we all die earlier, because we've got all this internal stress, because of the rules society puts on us that are really not realistic.
Neal

Men are perhaps on guard also because their sexuality is at times not gender specific. "Any port in a storm" may become the rationale of an aroused male in an all-male environment like prison, or the military, especially if they are the active rather than the passive one in a sexual act. They may feel, even in the homogenital act, that their masculinity and heterosexuality remains uncompromised because they are simply gratifying a natural male "need." Those who might otherwise be very threatened in their masculinity by such an act may feel somewhat redeemed that they have been at the same time contemptuous and/or dominating, and possibly abusive, of the one with whom they have committed the act. The extreme form of this is homosexual rape, something once commonly practiced by warriors against their vanquished, and against unwelcome strangers, especially if of another race or clan. This is the threat of the men of Sodom against Lot's "guests."

At a time when men are feeling disoriented and disempowered in their roles, gay pride and gay liberation seem to some of them a subversive action, a betrayal of male identity. That perhaps accounts for much of the gay bashing, and even for the murder of Matthew Shepherd. But some heterosexual men are finding that gay liberation also works out to be a liberation for them. They can find a new identity that is not based simply on the need to assert and defend male dominance. It allows them to have more emotionally rich lives, and to be more fully themselves.

Chapter 10

Getting it Straight

"I looked up 'left hand,' and it said, see 'right hand.'"

I am a left-handed man in right-handed world. It's tolerable - easily so. I live at a time and in a place where left handedness is not only tolerated, it is accepted. That was not always true everywhere, and may not be true everywhere today. Many years ago, addressing an envelop in a post office in Germany, my hand was wrapped around like most left-handers, almost like I was writing upside down. An elderly woman gave me long disapproving glances and finally said, "You're mother should have taught you how to write." Being left-handed, though a light burden, does perhaps give one a small measure of empathy with those whose natures do not run altogether with the grain of the world. One is acquainted with the easy presumption of those who are right-handed that the table of this world should be set to their nature and their convenience. Gays are the left-handed in a right-handed world in a far more significant sense.

Knowing at least a couple of instances where the left hand is mentioned in the Bible, I looked to find other references. In <u>The Interpreter's Dictionary of the Bible</u>, under "left hand," I found only three words, "see right hand." Being left-handed, I was a bit startled and offended. It was as though a woman looked up "Eve" and found only, "see Adam," or as if a gay man looked up "homosexual" and found only, "see heterosexual." Are some people in their nature to be defined only as the opposite, or as a derivative, of another?

Handedness, like the grain in a piece of wood, the direction a river flows, or the way the world rotates, is a given - an orientation. Because there are far more heterosexuals than homosexuals, some assume that heterosexuality is therefore natural and homosexuality is unnatural, and thereby unholy. On the same basis one could say that it is natural to be a brunet and unnatural - and unholy - to be a redhead.

In a right-handed world there is a real, but unspoken, sense that this reflects the bias of a creator who is "himself" right-handed. The *righteous* will sit on God's *right* hand. What is right-handed is what to most people seems normal, appropriate, natural, and yes - "right." The word "righteous" partakes of the bias toward things on the right. A "self-righteous" person is one who attributes to himself or herself the qualities that they believe comprise goodness, which are generally the values of dominant and prevailing culture. Those on God's left hand are those who are in some relative sense apart from handedness - on the left, out of sinc, outlaw. They may be of the "left" politically and ideologically, a despised quality to those who politically and ideologically are on the "right."

I am not suggesting, of course, that clocks, which turn to the right, should be refaced so that they move "counterclockwise," or that we in the Western world should read to the left rather than the right, that a revolving door should turn to the left rather than the right, or that a table setting should be reversed. What we do need is an awareness that the way a majority is oriented in this world, though it may "rightly" suggest a way of designing something for maximum, if not universal, convenience, does not establish what is good, or natural.

As it is not unnatural for someone to be left-handed, so also it is not unnatural for someone to be homosexual. These are the natures of a minority but a very significant number of persons. A majority is not indicative of a divine preference. Jesus came to love, call, heal, and pronounce salvation to those who in every sense are on God's left as well as right hand. Jesus paid specific attention, and called attention to, the worth of minorities. In the parable of the lost sheep, the one percent matters as much as the ninety nine percent. That's a fairly radical and sometimes dangerous idea now as it was then.

Those on God's left hand are like the ones the English writer, Colin Wilson, identified a number of years ago (1987) as "outsider" personalities. Using again, if I may, the analogy of handedness - like the left-handed persons seated at a formal dinner table, the very things that accommodate and make right-handed persons comfortable are the ones that make the left-handed persons uncomfortable and looking awkward. Especially there is the possibility that their elbows are going to collide with the elbows of the right-handed person next to them; and it is the left-handed person who feels impelled to apologize for the problem. They are the odd one, the queer one, the one out of sync. So in life more generally, the ones on God's left hand are somewhat expected to defer in various ways, if not to be actually apologetic for who they are, to those on God's right hand. These presumptions are ones that many people live by in politics, and religion, and a variety of human affairs.

Many conservatives in this country argue that they represent prevailing culture, are a moral majority, and therefore, what they believe should be what is taught in public schools and be the standard of law and ethics throughout the land. They see politics as a "winner take all enterprise." President George Bush, who became president with a minority of the popular vote, and barely squeaked out a victory in Ohio to gain his second term, declared after that election that he had a mandate and was going to use it.

The Australian film, "Strictly Ballroom," is a kind of parable of the "outsider" personality. It is about a man who is part of a tight ethnic community, Greek, and the rising star of the Society of Ballroom Dancers. He falls from grace in that society because he introduces "new steps," which are drawn from his ethnic heritage, into the traditional "orthodox" style of ballroom dancing.

The very boundaries inherent to a "right-handed world" are the boundaries that others must cross to be themselves. Those who I refer to as being "on God's left hand" are often, therefore, the boundary breakers, for good and for ill, in history. The Bible tells the stories of many boundary breakers. Abraham, Joseph, Moses, and various prophets are persons marked by their having left one place to arrive at another, opposed prevailing law or culture or, like Joseph, were cast out or sold out. The Hebrews themselves evolved as a distinct people because of their experiences of exile, exodus, and captivity, though their experiences were also because they were, and often chose to be, a people with a distinct and exclusive cultural identity. They were often persons who were aliens where they lived. Something happened to these persons that put them, so to speak, outside the gate, outside the village wall. From there they experienced the world differently than did those "inside." They were not those to whom belonging, acceptance, power, and affirmation came as the norms of this life. They seem not to be the persons for whom the table of this world is set. The circumstances of their lives, if not the innate nature of their being, caused them either to be driven outside the gate or to choose to go beyond it.

The Gospels are filled with "outsiders" and Jesus is forever seeing them, addressing them, healing, touching, receiving, and embracing them, and totally without condescension, and with only such judgment as is necessary to engage them in their own redemptive process. Jesus always took on the perspective of the disadvantaged, despised, or abused, (*...just as you did it to one of the least of these who are members of my family, you did it to me."* Matthew 25:40). Whether one is a fundamentalist or a Unitarian, this observation about Jesus can only be escaped by those determined not to see what is as apparent as the sky.

The Gospels open with a portrait of a man totally other than the establishment type of his time or any other time - John the Baptist. Though perhaps not as austere as John, the disciples seem to be an unusual lot in their willingness to cut loose of conventional expectations to follow Jesus. This small band of men is diverse and includes both a zealot and a tax collector, who one would expect to be natural adversaries, one opposing the Roman occupation and the other colluding with them. They are persons willing to make an extraordinary commitment to leave one place to arrive at some other, largely unknown, destination.

The God revealed in Jesus Christ is an ambidextrous God, as left-handed as right-handed, as female as male. Those on God's left hand are as near as those on the right, and the one is as honored as the other, and also is as culpable as the other. There is no odd nor even. The prodigal is as loved as his older brother, and the daughter as loved as the son.

It isn't as though the Bible never mentions God's left hand. I could immediately think of two instances; the mother of James and John lobbying Jesus to allow her sons to sit one on Jesus' right hand and the other on his left (Matthew 20:20-22), and where Jesus speaks of the sorting out in the last days, and of the sheep being placed on his right hand and the goats on his left (Matthew 25:31-46). In the Matthew 25 passage; to be on God's right hand is an honored position and to be on God's left a position of shame. Although left hand gets a very unfavorable treatment here, what is especially significant is that those who are self-righteous about their religiosity, and no doubt consider themselves to be on God's right hand, are the ones put on God's left hand.

The mother of James and John (Salome) was looking out for her sons when she tried to get the most honored places for them. She wanted one to sit on Jesus' right and the other on his left hand in the kingdom of heaven, no doubt because she had two sons and perceived God to have only one right hand (though God, being God, is perhaps omnihanded). In this instance, if the right hand is the most honored position, the left hand seems at least second best. What, I wonder, was the protocol for the seating of the disciples at the last supper?

We extend our right hand to shake hands, and we put our right hand over our heart to say the pledge of allegiance. In giving testimony witnesses are instructed to "raise their right hand and swear...," Would the testimony be less credible if they raised their left hand? A left-handed compliment is one with a nasty twist in it. The most isolated place to be in a baseball game, or in life, is out in left field.

The author of Leviticus is fixated with what is clean and unclean, and quite understandably so, given the rigors of life - especially nomadic life - in the ancient world. Clean and unclean took on a religious connotation with circumcision, dietary laws, foot washing, and baptism. The practical realities of hygiene were turned into a religious obsession. That obsession in the early Church was initially the rationale for the exclusion of Gentiles. The uncircumcised were presumed to be unclean. That is addressed in the story of Peter and Cornelius in the 10th chapter of Acts. In Matthew's gospel, Jesus is blisteringly critical of the hypocritical nature of the Scribes and Pharisees for their obsession with exterior cleanliness; "....*You clean the outside of cup and dish, which you have filled inside by robbery and self-indulgence! Blind Pharisees! Clean the inside of the cup first, then the outside will be clean also.*" (Matthew 23:25-26)

The concept of clean and unclean has of course much to do with attitudes about homosexuality today, especially between men. Male homosexuality is often identified with sodomy. There are several assumptions in that which are frequently incorrect. One is that sodomy has only one meaning, anal sex, and that it is practiced only by homosexuals. Another assumption is that this is the only or primary way male homosexuals relate. Strangely, most of the sodomy laws in various states in this country (now struck down by the Supreme Court) applied only to same sex couples not to heterosexual couples.

In the popular parlance of sexual orientation there are two categories; gay and straight. In our society the word "straight" has a moral connotation of good - a straight-thinker, a straight arrow, a straight shooter, straight and true. The word "orthodox," which means straight, is the religious version of the generic term. Those Protestant denominations often called "*mainline*" are orthodox - therefore straight in their theology. There are other terms commonly used which rank certain things, generally on the basis of majority. "*Major*" is treated as better than minor - in baseball; and many other enterprises. A major key is one stronger and more dominant than a minor one. "*Regular*" is better than irregular. "*Irregular*" on merchandise means "defective" and costs less. Several years ago when the church where I was pastor ordained a gay man as elder, the Presbytery (the regional judicatory) brought a charge against us of having committed an "irregularity." "*Normal*" is an affirmation, while "*abnormal*" and "*queer*" are terms of derision. Similarly, *"right"* has a more positive connotation than *"left."* In Latin, left means sinister, and in French it means gauche. No one is referred to as someone's "left-hand man," and it wouldn't be taken as a compliment if they were (although I have noticed that when Queen Elizabeth processes down a church aisle her husband is on her left; apparently in that instance rank takes precedence over gender).

In our culture one often hears of the values of *"middle"* America, or of the American *"heartland."* George Bush took his second month-long vacation in the first seven months of his presidency at his ranch in Crawford, Texas. To avert criticism he billed the vacation as spending time in the "heartland." It implied a kind of Abe Lincoln type guy who wanted to be in close touch with "real people," even though the real people of Crawford were not likely to catch more than a distant glimpse of him. But something about that word "heartland" conveys the solid, the real, the moral, even the beautiful America. This is Grant Wood's "American Gothic." Here it seems implied that people live by God-given values. What would we consider the values of coastal America to be - say, San Francisco or New York City? Or of northern industrial America - Chicago or Detroit? Southern America is associated with values similar to those of middle America. For the most part in our minds, these values are those of rural and small town America as opposed to urban and industrial America.

Straight, orthodox, mainline, rightminded, major, regular, normal, middle, and heartland - these all have similar and related meanings. These are the highways, not the byways, of culture. Words are not as benign as they sometimes seem. They identify the more acceptable way - if not Paul's "more excellent way." These are the templates of our culture. These are the main roads, the way the river runs, the grain - if not of this world - of this culture. The message is, go with the flow and you will go farther and faster. This all gets learned subconsciously quite early in life.

Persons do not usually think of any of these terms as pejorative or condescending. Consider the term often used now even by some progressive persons about the lives of gays - "an alternate life style." It is an alternative to what? Do they mean an alternative to their life style which is "straight?" Do they mean an alternative to the main thing? the accepted thing? the "right" and proper thing? Some persons try to show their tolerance by saying they accept persons who have "an alternate life style." That is a kind of "left-handed" tolerance. Does anyone ever speak of heterosexuality as an "alternate life style?" If the term alternating means "this way" then "that way" of things that are relatively equal, then heterosexuality is also an alternate lifestyle, but I doubt that any heterosexuals think of it that way. This is most often problematic for gays - and their children if they have them - when others refer to their relationships as an *alternative family*. Their family is their family, it is not an alternative to someone else's family.

In England, the focus of the gay/lesbian issue politically was for a long while something called "article 28," passed during the Thatcher administration. Addressed to public school education it said that they could not teach as proper "pretended families" of same sex couples. The term outraged liberals and progressives in England and has been repealed, but the offending term was uncomfortably close to the one used here - alternative families.

Some persons express their tolerance by being "politically correct," which becomes a craft in itself. It has a humorous side as revealed in what may be a particularly well remembered episode of "Seinfeld." In their customary restaurant booth some clowning around between Jerry and George is overheard by a young woman in a neighboring booth causing her to believe - mistakenly - that they are a gay couple. When they become aware that the young woman thinks they are gay, both men are somewhat panicked that their heterosexual image is endangered. Denying that they are gay and at the same time trying to remain politically correct whenever the term "gay" comes up, they quickly say, "*not that there is anything wrong with that.*" Among self-conscious liberals, "political correctness" sometimes becomes a tedious art form. Real change will be evident, of course, when our language is simply a reflection of a just society rather than guarded speech. However, our path to that may require a high degree of intentionality.

In life, if the only way we will take is the broad straight highway, there are many vistas we will never see. If I drive from Los Angeles to San Francisco, I have a choice to make. If I go over the Grapevine and straight up highway 5, I can make very good time on a broad mostly straight highway. It will be a faster though not a very eventful trip. If however I go up highway 1, I will go along the lovely coast south and north of Santa Barbara, and where it turns inland I will drive through the beautiful Santa Inez Valley. I might even stop in the picturesque Danish town of Solvang for lunch, then drive along the ocean again to Pismo Beach. North from San Luis Obispo I will go through some hills, and if I'm really committed to enjoying my trip, I can then take for 90 miles the very winding coastal road of old highway 1 that goes through Big Sur and along one of the most spectacular coastlines in the world. I will see the vivid colors of iceplant that spill over the ocean rocks along the Monterey Peninsula. After driving along more ocean beaches I will come into San Francisco with a view of the Golden Gate.

The "straight" way is not the only way worth taking. If the only music we will listen to must be in major keys, there is great music we will never hear.

I happened to grow up in a family where individualism and diversity were valued and affirmed. Diversity was affirmed because there was, among five children, so much of it. There were rules we understood for maintaining our diversity. One of those was that you could get mad, argue and shout and alarm the neighbors, but you also had to get over it, and soon. Voltaire's words were often quoted ponderously, though sometimes grudgingly, among us in the heat of argument: *"I may not agree with what you have to say, but I will defend to the death your right to say it."* We were sort of odd ball and would say melodramatic things like that.

As a child I seemed to believe that other families were like my own and that children were raised to respect diversity. By the time I was in Junior High School I was aware that we were perhaps the exception more than the rule, and that what most children learned growing up was how to find where the main roads were and how to follow them. I learned that there was a certain hierarchy of values that was deep but not wide. Parents were anxious that in every way their children be perceived as "normal." In small towns that was especially important. Families had to consider their reputation and place within that kind of community, where anonymity was not easy, especially if one was or did anything out of the ordinary, good or bad.

Culture has grooves. These grooves, in fact, define the culture. The world is generally not kind to those who live outside these grooves, one of which is heterosexism. To quote again the anonymous friend whose story is in Chapter 1: *"...the lessons from my past breed caution, for there lurks in all of us an incipient intolerance toward difference, that, like the spark of tinder under the right conditions, can start again the flames of violence and hatred."*

Not just in matters of sexuality, but with any nonconformity, a small town can be toxic for a child. In 1970 Dick Cavett did an interview with Janis Joplin where she talked about a journey she was about to make back to the town in Texas where she had grown up.

Cavett: *"Did you ever get back to Port Arthur, Texas?"*
Janis: *"No, but I'm going back next in August, man. And guess what I'm doin'?"*
Cavett: *"I don't know."*
Janis: *"I'm going to my 10th annual High School reunion.*
Cavett: *"Oh! Oh! Take movies and bring 'em back to show, will you?"*
Janis: "Hey would you like to go?"
Cavett: *"Well, I don't remember....I don't have any friends in your high school class."*
Janis: *"I don't either. I don't either, believe me."*
Cavett: *"You don't either?"*
Janis: *"It's hard going (back), man!"*
Cavett: (trying to remember something he had heard or read) *"Weren't you a kind of a...weren't you kind of a business administration major or something in high school. No, it's something in your past., you were...."*
Janis: *"No, I worked."*
Cavett: *"Yeah?"*
Janis: *"But a high school major in arts does have plenty of time."*
Cavett: *"Yeah, and do you think you'll have a lot to say to your old high-school classmates?"*
Janis: *"I don't have a lot, man."*
Cavett: *"You were not surrounded by friends in high school?"*

Janis: *"They laughed me out of class, out of town, and out of the state, man."*

About to return as a rock star clearly held for her both triumph and great pain. Her untimely death came shortly after this, (In the movie "The Rose" with Bette Midler, based on Janis Joplin, this return to her hometown is the climax of the film).

In the small town where I grew up, and perhaps in most small towns, people thought of themselves as "tolerant" of gay and lesbian persons so long as they did not make demands that upset the orderly, and moral, arrangement - as they perceived it - of society. Tolerance itself is condescending as it implies some forbearance of the strong toward the weak, the normal toward the abnormal, or the morally straight toward the morally defective.

The unwritten but understood social contract was that you could live in a community and be generally accepted, even appreciated for whatever contribution you made to the life of that community, so long as you were never open about your sexual orientation, and so long as you never "pretended" that your relationship with someone you loved was in any sense comparable to that of married persons.

I'm aware of a high school music teacher and bandleader who lived decades in a small town, was widely known among those in the community and appreciated for the well-drilled and spiffy high school band which sort of put this small town "on the map" throughout the state. He was a gay man, which most folks in the town either knew or suspected. He lived with another male high school teacher. He followed the unwritten rule of his time: never demand nor expect that your life can be lived as others live their lives. That is a story that would have belonged to thousands, perhaps millions, in American towns before the

Stonewall rebellion. It is no doubt the story of many gay persons today.

The particular attitudes in my family, I believe, had something to do with my mother shaking off the conservatism of her Iowa upbringing and taking off to live in Montana, which in the 1920's was still a fairly rustic environment. Over the years I have found that there is something markedly different about those persons who "got up and left" and those who stayed. For twenty years, I served a small congregation in Southern California that was made up largely of transplanted Midwesterners, some of whom came with their parents because of the dust bowl, or others to work in defense plants, the packing houses or vineyards, and others came simply for the sun and to put their feet in the ocean. They were - and are - a very different kind of cat, a can-do people. For decades that feisty little congregation has stood up for the disempowered of every variety not so much because of political ideology but because they have a natural respect for diversity and individualism.

Those who leave one place and journey to another are somewhat different than those who stay at home. We find this is in the parable of the prodigal son and his elder brother. Those who journey have a different spiritual experience, and a particular reliance on God. To journey is to enlarge one's experience of diversity which increases one's capacity for empathy.

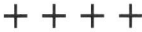

To be inclusive, the Church must first have a theology of inclusiveness and, behind that, a spirit of inclusiveness. It is not in our structures - but first in our hearts - that we are inclusive. What is in our hearts is in how we see, how we experience God. Some simple observation might lead us nearer to the heart of God. In the parable of the great banquet when the invited guests do not arrive, the host instructs the stewards to "*go out to the highways and hedges, and compel people to come in, that my house may be filled.*" (Luke 14:16-24) Sticking to the main roads, the broad highways, the Church for the most part has a theology of exclusiveness, and behind that a spirit of exclusiveness. She is uncomfortable with diversity and non-conformity. It strikes me that whoever does not believe that God loves diversity must never have been to the zoo. However, that which calls itself "mainline" is not into diversity and inclusiveness. It's almost an oxymoron.

As one who was a pastor in local churches for thirty two years, I am neither unmindful, nor naive about the predicament faced by churches, especially mainline churches, in relation to the issues involving gay and lesbian persons. Nor am I unsympathetic to the problems they face. Those problems exist not just in attitudes but in the structures themselves.

Pastors are seldom prophets, and prophets are seldom pastors. A very high price is generally paid by prophets for their freedom of movement and speech, and their followers are apt to be small and maverick on their own. Yet they play an important role in envisioning what the Church should be and challenging it to rise to that vision. Pastors, however, especially of mainline churches, have a high degree of accountability to their congregations and to their denomination at large. Even when their own hearts are in the right place - and many are - there are practical realities that inhibit their prophetic voice.

There is an entrepreneurial spirit in the Church. Churches want to grow. Whether that is worldly or not, they do tend to measure the "success" of their ministry in that way. But also their ministries exist to reach and serve all that they can. Moreover, to carry out that mission they have the burden of being financially viable.

Pastors face those realities. To alienate a segment of the congregation and thereby create controversy in the life of the Church seems to many to undermine the mission of that church and threaten its viability. That threat is existential for pastors who, besides having a natural desire to be successful professionally, probably have a mortgage, a family to support, and children to put through college. They know their own expendability. Very often the support of whatever governing body is over a local church is directed more toward the congregation, and the pastors are forced to seek a new call for the sake of the "peace and unity" of that local church. And they must do so with the taint of being the pastors of local congregations that are divided. These realities tend toward their overvaluing of patience and their undervaluing of courage. They hope that somehow time alone will bring change. But they often fail to see that the time they are taking is not their own, but is other persons' lives - passing.

It should also be acknowledged that the attitudes that now stymie the Church on this issue are ones that, in the past, or in some instances in the present, the Church itself has generated. They are reaping what they sowed. There is a failure of leadership on this issue and the reasons for that go deep.

It might surprise many parishioners to know what their pastors did not learn in seminary. Human sexuality, though it should have been, was generally not part of the curriculum (not even as an elective course). And one might ask, if it were, who would teach it and what would their qualifications need to be? Seminaries and Christian colleges are somewhat constrained in their curriculum design and hiring of faculty by the alumni, donors, and denominations that support them. Few therefore, especially if their support comes from conservatives, are adventuress in these areas.

Out of seminary the newly ordained pastor is apt to become instantly a marriage and family counselor, a counselor of youth, of the about-to-be-married, the sick, the aging, and those that mourn. Parishioners assume that they have had the professional training necessary for these roles. Usually they haven't. The bulk of seminary training is in scripture, theology, church history, preaching, and worship, and very little in the arts of pastoral care.

In the beginning of their ministries, many pastors are simply untrained and inexperienced, though perhaps they have had some mentoring by an older more experienced pastor. When a pastor is dealing with issues of human sexuality - straight, gay, or otherwise - they are generally operating simply out of their own personal beliefs and experience. That experience is often quite limited, especially in their having any great knowledge about gay persons.

Change is not apt to come spontaneously out of these structures. Change will likely come only as the Church is forced to respond to the moral evolution of society at large, or in response to a catalytic event. For a while one hoped that the AIDS epidemic, or the murder of Matthew Shepherd and other hate crimes, would deeply penetrate the conscience of the Church. But for the most part, the Church has weathered these with little more than some occasional compassionate rhetoric or giving some financial support toward medical missions relating to the AIDS crisis in Africa. Though this support is enormously needed, throughout my life it has seemed that foreign mission has had particular appeal. It is difficult not to suspect sometimes that the appeal has much to do with its being foreign. Compassion and justice nearer to home meets sometimes with great resistance, especially justice.

Chapter 11

Searching for Texas

Gloria: *"Face it daddy, you're just afraid of sex."*
Archie: *"I am not afraid of...of...that."*
Meathead (Michael): *"See, you can't even say the word."*
Archie: (turning to Gloria) *"Listen little girl, if I was
   afraid of it you wouldn't even be here."*
Meathead: *"Gloria's right,* (to Edith)
   When was the last time you and Archie made love?"
Archie: (After a long pause with all eyes turned
   toward Edith who seems lost in thought.) *"W-e-ll?"*
Edith: *"I'm trying to remember."*
as recalled from an episode
of "All in the Family"

     For many Christians, some churches, and even whole denominations, trying to deal with homosexuality is like a person trying to get to Dallas but unable thus far to find Texas. The Church's failure to address homosexuality consistently, compassionately, and theologically is not isolated but resides in an inability, or reluctance, to deal with issues of human sexuality overall. That sends a message to the individual, gay or straight, trying to understand and cope with his or her sexual feelings. It says, *"you had better look somewhere else than the Church in dealing with this."*
     "Homosexuality" is an unfortunate term which only came into existence in the 19th century. It is unfortunate because it tends to focus the diverse and complex elements of persons' lives on just one aspect of those lives, and unfortunate because anything related to sex seems to come with a built in exclamation mark related to persons' overall

anxiety about sexuality. "Gay," however much some persons do not like that term, is a better one simply because it conveys a more wholistic view of others.

The term "gay" has evolved into having both a generic and a gender specific use. It sometimes refers to all homosexuals and sometimes to only male homosexuals, as many homosexual women prefer to be identified as lesbian, distinguishing themselves from male homosexuals. Although I favor using the terminology that persons choose to identify themselves rather than the terminology chosen by others, we seem, unfortunately, to be stuck with the terms, homosexuality and heterosexuality, for much of the discussion of these issues. The development of language lags behind social change.

Though in my denomination, and it is no doubt similar in other mainline denominations, some attempts have been made to address the wider issues of human sexuality, little if any progress has been made. Presbyterians have periodically made forays into this subject matter with special commissions or task forces. When those assigned to this mission report to the denomination with their carefully and prayerfully thought out recommendations, their work is either rejected outright, sanitized, shelved, or referred to a committee for its gradual demise.

In 1998 The General Assembly of the Presbyterian Church USA (the annual national legislative gathering of the denomination) met in Albuquerque, New Mexico. It had special significance for gay and lesbian Presbyterians because the commissioners to that assembly, after years of controversy, formally voted to put into their constitution, the Book of Order, a rule prohibiting the ordination of persons as Ministers of the Word (clergy), Elders or Deacons, those who are *"unrepentant and practicing"* homosexuals. The most operative phrase was that only those living "...*in fidelity in marriage between a man and a woman or chastity in singleness,"* could be ordained. That meant, in the minds of many, that any living "as married" in committed same-sex relationships were prohibited since the church, refusing to recognize those relationships, regarded them as single but not chaste. The exact meaning of the phrase relies on the definition of the word "chastity", and on that there is less than unanimity. The Church did put some constraints on itself against any unwarranted or random investigation into the private lives of their members (probably more because this would violate heterosexuals in the denomination than because it would violate those who are gay).

Ironically those gays most in jeopardy in the denomination were those living openly and honestly in committed relationships. Such a relationship, many held, was itself evidence enough of their being in violation of this article or at least gave grounds for an inquiry into the "sexual practice" of those persons.

The denomination, being deeply divided on this faced floor debate that was vigorous. As the report came to the whole assembly, it defined marriage as being, *"between one man and one woman,"* purposely excluding its being between two men or two women. A commissioner rose to move that this be amended to say *"a man and a woman."* Everyone present, I think, knew the intent of the amendment was so as to not offend divorced and remarried persons, of which, of course, there are many in local congregations. The amendment passed.

Heterosexuals, even while denigrating the love relationships of gays, knew how to protect others more acceptable to them from any offense related to their love relationships. Though I don't object to the amendment, I was impressed with heterosexuals' gift to accommodate themselves in the same action which placed a cruel burden on others. After all, Jesus never said a word about same-sex relationships, though he spoke with unmistakable clarity about divorce, primarily, I believe, because of the destitute situation it would likely create for a woman in that patriarchal culture. I am sometimes amazed that persons who consistently appeal to the maintenance of "Biblical standards" have such agility in getting around whatever in scripture gets in the way of their own priorities.

Near the close of debate a commissioner stood up and asked the chairwoman of the committee presenting the overture, *"Does this ("...chastity in singleness") include masturbation?"* It was a serious question deserving a serious answer, but it never got one from her. Instead, the question produced fluster and embarrassed laughter. Some of those who didn't laugh probably thought the question improper, even shocking. Others, thankfully, didn't laugh, because they recognized the question as both appropriate and relevant.

The woman chairing the committee, clearly uncomfortable with the question, deferred to the Stated Clerk, whose role is to clarify the meaning of overtures. Being serious, he could only answer that the overture itself simply did not specify if it included masturbation. Had this not been explicitly about something sexual there probably would have been those pressing for the question to be addressed either by the chairwoman or others on the committee that had written the overture. But the General Assembly almost immediately thereafter moved to vote on the report. Another reason the Assembly no doubt "hurried on by" this question was that it had implications for heterosexual as well as homosexual persons. The question could have drawn us all into the real world, but the Assembly wasn't going there.

While writing this book, I have felt some timidity of my own regarding the open discussion of issues of human sexuality. Since I am ordained I am aware that many persons may tend to think this rite has a neutering effect. It is not my nature to want to make other persons feel uncomfortable, and I know how easily some do feel discomfort over any open discussion of sexuality, homosexuality especially. One can usually feel others discomfort in various forums of the church where these issues arise. I have sat with amazement in meetings of church judicatories that were debating issues of human sexuality and the word "sex" never was openly spoken. Everything was framed in euphemisms or reference numbers in our Book of Order (constitution). *"It's how Presbyterians talk about sex,"* says Rev. Katy Morrison, whose ministry is directed toward creating inclusive congregations. When you see persons going out of their way not to say the words aloud, you know there is a problem. That is not a problem of course just with homosexuality but with all of human sexuality.

When my son was about eleven or twelve we went one afternoon to the matinee of a movie that turned out to be a bit steamier than I had expected. I must have seemed rather tense as a particular scene began to be fairly sexually explicit, because my son put his hand reassuringly on my shoulder - as if to let me know *he* could handle it - and said, *"are you all right dad?"*

Part of the divide between generations, where there is one, is that those born in the last three decades are not nearly as uncomfortable with this issue as many of those in the generations ahead of them. Even the fact that adolescents today are more comfortable talking about sex, causes parents to fear they may be more comfortable also in having sex. In some measure they are. Statistical evidence seems to indicate that they may not necessarily be more likely than their parents during adolescence to have sex, but they probably experience less shame than their parents if they do; and general social disapproval will not be as great as when those of my generation were adolescents. The influence of films, TV, and general public discourse has no doubt played a major role in changing attitudes.

Past adolescence, partly because they tend to marry later, many of the younger generation are certainly more comfortable in living with someone before they are married. The church for the most part knows this and tries to act and legislate as though it isn't really happening. Despite the denomination's statement about "chastity in singleness," many, if not most couples being married have been intimate, and many of them have been living together. In over thirty five years of pastoral ministry I officiated at the weddings of perhaps two to three hundred couples. In very few of those instances were the bride and groom virgins, though their only sexual experience may have been with each other. Most ministers in this or other denominations would likely acknowledge the same to be true with couples they have married. These relationships are as apt to exist for those who self-designate themselves as conservative or evangelical, as they are for others.

Many Christians find it difficult to be face-to-face with gay and lesbian persons in any context where sexuality might be discussed. The inability to be face-to-face with them allows so called, "straight" persons to project their own version of these persons lives, relationships, life style, and spirituality. Much of that is false, distorted, or naive. But mostly, it is abstract. It sees the issue but not the person. Perhaps the deepest sin committed against gay and lesbian persons is the depersonalization of them.

To just identify the fear behind this phenomena as homophobia is too simplistic. The fear is that to look at any aspect of human sexuality deeply is a passageway into a dark and frightening world where people do not want to go. In our post-Freudian world, this fear is not surprising. Sexuality is the theater of the mind (mostly the subconscious), for it is the place of acting out our longings, needs, hurts, desires, and fantasies. Our whole being, body, mind, and spirit - senses, thoughts, and emotions - are drawn into our sexuality. The idea that we can separate our sexuality from our lives overall is the most desperate of hopes. And where the drive to make that separation exists, its origin is fear; and that fear is related to the depth and power of our sexuality. Our sexuality is something like a mysterious icon on our computer, perhaps, we fear, a virus. If we "open it," what will we find? what will happen?

Like the ocean, human sexuality is something totally essential to our being, yet it remains a frightening frontier to explore. In that depth is darkness (*"...and darkness was on the face of the deep..."* Genesis 1:2) and that darkness, we fear, may be inhabited by frightening creatures. There lies Leviathan.

"The Biblical allusions to leviathan (Psalm. 74:14, Isaiah 27:1) *are part of an almost universal mythology in which a monster, symbolic of evil, is contended against but is ultimately defeated by the power of good."*

(Harper's Bible Dictionary)

Everyday, everywhere, in everyone, like the ocean, this dimension exists, sometimes tranquil and sometimes turbulent. Marriage, that is heterosexual marriage, is seen by many as the only safe harbor.

Today there are hardly any TV sitcoms or dramas that do not explore somewhere within them, gay themes. There are many films as well, so much so that there are now gay film festivals annually in most major cities. Some think that is because there is considerable gay influence in these industries. A more likely reason is that these themes are often compelling, opening up the endless exploration of what it means to be male and female and the complexities of human relationships. This exploration is work the Church, by and large, is unwilling to do.

The Church wants to promote itself as a guide and a guard of morality, but in many ways, and on the issue of homosexuality especially, it does not lead; it follows. Perhaps this is no different than it has ever been. The artists, writers, philosophers, and poets of every age tend to lead in the moral evolution of the culture. Today that would include filmmakers. "Brokeback Mountain" may have had more impact on social consciousness than anything the Church has done related to this issue in more than 30 years. Artists and writers are often the avant guard, and the Church often vigorously resists their exploration. When the risks have been taken by others, the Church, in time, may find its own self-interest there. Then it will come in to do the settling and the integrating of the frontier that has been opened by others.

Despite its uneven pace, and sometimes backward steps, some progress has been made on the moral front. Fundamentalists generally, of course, do not like the concept of evolution and feel that we should only look back to see what is moral, rather than to look forward. If I look back, as they do, we seem not always to be seeing the same things.

Many fundamentalists believe, or at least speak as though they believe, that their views regarding sexual morality are taken directly from the Bible. But so much of what they believe simply is not there. If we could break free of the cultural bias by which we read scripture, we would likely see that almost immediately. The moral judgments we find in scripture relate to procreation, to patriarchal culture and to Jewish exclusivism. The Old Testament is filled with polygamy, and through the patriarchal period, incest. The Old Testament "heroes," provide no model of fidelity or abstinence. Adultery applied only if a man went outside his marriage, or marriages, to have sex with some other man's wife (property).

Fornication, being the Biblical "f" word, has a nasty sound. We are inclined to think its meaning is simply promiscuity, "sleeping around," but the Biblical meaning is a little more complex than that. For a man to have sex with a woman, even if she were unmarried, it almost always meant he was having a sexual relationship with some other person's property, that of her father, or brother, or closest male kin. Fornication was to have intercourse with an unmarried woman, presumably a virgin, possibly impregnating her and totally diminishing the value of her father's "property" without compensating him for it, and leaving her destitute. It wasn't condemned simply because it was sex; it had great social implications.

In the New Testament there is huge silence about sexual practice, which doesn't mean there wasn't any. Among Jesus' followers, some chose celibacy. Paul viewed marriage in an eschatological context and saw it largely as an encumbrance to the evangelical mission. Jesus was open and kind and remarkably non-judgmental toward persons in this regard, though he spoke forcefully against divorce. Polygamy, though less practiced, lasted well past the New Testament era.

The reality is that however much individuals may fail to live up to it, the standards of sexual morality that guide us in this culture are based not on a lower but a higher ethic than is found in much of the Bible. They are more grounded in the worth and inviability of all persons. In most of scripture sexual practice was based on ownership, and it says almost nothing about what sort of sexual practice was allowable. Being based on ownership, it is likely that the practice was often abusive.

I am a romantic, as are most people in this culture, in believing that a sexual ethic based on romantic love, equality and mutuality is the right ethic. Though clearly difficult for many to sustain, we still believe that is the context most beneficial to the individual and to the human race. It is one toward which we have evolved over centuries. But its origin in the Bible is only in Israel's evolution toward an ethic of love and justice that ultimately leads toward that being the most meaningful context for a sexual relationship.

The ideal of romantic love came to the fore in such stories as the medieval legend of "Tristan and Iseult," and in the real life tragic love story of Abelard and Heloise (12th Century). Having arrived where romantic love in Western society is the basis of marriage and the foundation of the family, we also have ended up with a kind of sexual imperialism. Heterosexual persons who married claimed this sexuality as their divine right and demanded that whoever else claimed love and intimacy should be ostracized, ridiculed, or criminalized. Heterosexuality became part of the cultural definition of male and female, thereby identifying any persons of either of those genders who was not heterosexual as "queer," as malformed, and an aberration in the human race. To accept homosexuality and homosexuals as normal is for many persons nothing less than a redefining of reality.

The Judeo-Christian tradition is one founded in sexual shame from the Adam and Eve story forward. Could that be more obvious than in the New Testament authors' insistence that Jesus was born of a virgin? The idea that the incarnation could not happen, that God could not physically enter the world except through a virgin, has been made an essential tenet of the faith and very often a test of orthodoxy. Add to that in the Roman Catholic tradition that Mary herself, even though a virgin, could not be a pure vessel unless in some way in her own birth she had been immaculately conceived. The idea here is that we are born in sin because we were conceived in sin, conceived through sexual intercourse.

For those fixated on what is clean and unclean, one can understand their sense that sex is "dirty," and that even natural functions - a woman's menstruation and male emissions - required ritual cleansing. In whatever pertained to the holy, their minds were uncomfortable with the reality that the organs of sexual union and of conception and birth were the means of God's entering the world. Though they accepted his birth, they seem to have been compelled to "sanitize" - sanctify - it in whatever ways they could.

Heterosexuality might be for many as shame-based as homosexuality were it not that it receives a divine dispensation because it holds the possibility of procreation. Of course, there are today many ways, natural and unnatural, to circumvent that possibility, and such circumvention is near universal. In the Catholic tradition, that removes the justification for sex, and so the Church is opposed to any kind of birth control that does not leave open the possibility of conception. Most Protestants, after the Reformation, seemed to make their peace with non-procreative sex so long as it was between married persons of the opposite sex. Now, in relation to homosexuality, many who employ a variety of methods not to conceive, or are past the age where there is any real likelihood that they could conceive, want to justify their discrimination against gays on the basis that it is non-procreative.

Her attitudes about gays are the arterial sclerosis of the Church, her hardening of the arteries. It is blockage, and it is life-threatening. The Church is suffocating on her fears. What do you do when you have a lingering problem you cannot find a way to solve? Over time you start trying not to think about it. That is what much of the Church has done with homosexuality; she tries not to think about it. She has this formula answer. In my denomination it is "*....fidelity in marriage between a man and a woman, and chastity in singleness.*" When "chastity in singleness" applies to homosexual persons, single because they are not allowed to marry, the Church is very earnest about it, but when it applies to heterosexual persons there is a kind of wink. It would be difficult to find an instance where an administrative or judicial action has been brought against a church because they have ordained a heterosexual as elder or deacon who is single and not chaste, though across the denomination there are likely hundreds, if not thousands, of such persons. The Church's formula answer is no real answer, because she fears the consequences if she opens herself to any of the real complexities of the question. If your starting point is a dogmatic answer, then the only allowable question is one which fits with that answer.

"Why," some will demand, "does it all have to be about this one issue?" But the greater reality is that for centuries it has not been about this issue. This issue has been denied and evaded. It has been widely skirted and diligently avoided. For generations persons of minority sexual orientation have been pushed to the back of the line. For those who have ever stood in line at a bank, post office, or store, it is understood, in fairness, that eventually those who were at the back of the line will be at the front of it, with their turn to be recognized and served. A lot of those in our churches, seeing now that gay/lesbian/bisexual/transgender persons are now at the front of the line, want to set out a sign that says, "THIS WINDOW CLOSED - COME BACK TOMORROW." That isn't going to happen, and that is a message that is being sent by many gay, lesbian, bisexual, and transgender persons. If you close this window, some may return, but most will not be back tomorrow, nor will many of their families or friends. That is a lot of people who will seek other places and other ways of coping with their spiritual hunger.

It is no longer as if there is nowhere else to go. There is - out there - a virtual parallel universe which includes alternatives for a person's spiritual life. The Metropolitan Community Church is basically their own worldwide denomination. There are other welcoming churches and inclusive denominations such as the United Church of Christ.

Gays are connected as never before in history. They have their own web sites, periodicals, book stores, travel agencies, real estate companies, and almost every other conceivable business - worldwide, many with their universal symbol, a rainbow flag, in front. Not relying altogether on what may, or may not be provided by others, gays have their own medical centers, systems of social services, political organizations, museums, theaters, and philanthropies. They have not only their own community centers but virtually their own communities. They create their own welcome with pubs, clubs, hotels, resorts, retreat centers, and cruises. There are gay tennis, bowling, and baseball leagues, hiking, biking, and skiing clubs, and their own Olympics. Since no one is having a parade for them, they have their own parades. Yes, there is a gay sub-culture, in which of course not all gays participate to the same degree. That sub-culture is a response and a reflection of what many have experienced in the wider society which implicitly, and sometimes literally, has put out a sign saying, "faggots stay out!"

Parents can no longer be counted on to implement the Church's rejection of their children. Parents themselves have often been victims, being expected to choose between their religion and their child. In the past many, sadly, chose what their religion wrongly taught them and rejected their child. That is changing, and it, perhaps more than anything else, will change the Church. Many parents will attest that when their child came out of the closet, they went into it. But many of these mothers and fathers have refused to stay there. They have come out of their closet of shame to stand by their child and say in effect: *"If you abuse my child, you abuse me. You will have me to reckon with."*

Parents aroused in defense of their children are a formidable force. In almost any gay pride parade the loudest cheer goes up for the parents of gays who march in those parades. If the Church does not give parents real permission to love and support their children, the Church becomes the enemy, not the friend, of their family.

Persons like to use the term "homosexual life style." As is constantly pointed out, to almost no avail to those who cannot or will not hear, there is no "gay life-style," precisely because there are myriads of gay life styles, some of which do not even slightly resemble each other. The idea of a "gay life style" is part of how gays are depersonalized. I think many peoples' mental image of "the gay life style" has to do with their idea of what happens in a gay bar. The TV series "Queer As Folk" probably contributed to that image. People might be surprised what does, and does not happen in gay bars. That scene is, in any case, one that many gay persons are not interested in. More to the point, if it is fair to think of that as a gay "life style" then it would be equally fair to think of a straight singles bar as the "heterosexual life style."

    I was in London for a couple of weeks after attending a conference in Edinburgh sponsored by the Gay and Lesbian Christian Movement for those engaged in ministry to and with gays. Intending to write a paper on this experience, I decided I would try to find gays with whom I might have some conversation in London. I asked an Anglican priest whom I had met at the conference where I might find an "inclusive" worship service to attend on Sunday. He directed me to St. Ann's in Soho. Searching for this church, I found it beside a wonderful (perhaps Christopher Wren) steeple, which is about all that remains of the large original structure destroyed by the Nazis' blitzing of London. Besides being in a part of London with many gay establishments, designated by rainbow flags, this Church's primary connection with the gay community seems to be that it is the place where many took refuge after the bombing of a gay pub only a block away.

    A rainbow banner hangs over its doorway. A stocky young security guard at the door warmly greets each person going in. If they are carrying any sort of bag he requests courteously to look into it. There is a reason. This is "The Admiral Duncan," where on April 30, 1999, a man walked in and set a small bag on the floor and left. A patron said to the manager that someone had forgotten a bag. The manager went toward it to pick it up saying, jokingly to someone, "*maybe it's a bomb*." Then it went off, killing four people (one of them preborn), blowing the feet off of another, and severely injuring many others, including the manager. The bomb had been devised to be especially lethal by the planting of nails in it.

The four who were killed were a young man and woman who were to be married the next day, the four-month fetus she was carrying, and the person who was to be their best man. Of course, not everyone in a gay pub is necessarily gay and these that were killed were not even the intended victims of the bomb. The friendly security guard of whom I had been asking questions, pointed out the manager who was seated at the bar. He still wore a bandage over one ear.

The guard also pointed out a memorial that was mounted on the ceiling over where the bomb had been placed. It was a sort of wreath of twisted metal intertwined with small lights. Another piece of metal was ribboned through the wreath engraved as a memorial to those who died or were injured. For gays in England, the "Admiral Duncan" is what a wooden fence near Laramie, Wyoming is for gays in America.

Following another recommendation, I visited another gay establishment in London. It is a venerable old pub near Hyde Park and was within walking distance of the B&B where I was staying. It was, for me, an opportunity to connect with gays in this very cosmopolitan city. The nearest equivalent to an English pub we have, it seems to me, is not a bar but a Starbuck's, though the coffee house is without the beer and bitters. It was afternoon when I visited this pub, a time when patrons sort of lounge around, reading papers, visiting, or just having a drink on their way home from work. A number of them carried briefcases. I ordered a glass of juice and sat down in one of the small lounge-like seating areas. After a while, a man seated nearby struck up a conversation. I always found that the moment I opened my mouth, they knew I was an American, having, as I do, that "American accent." In fact this became something of the subject of our conversation as his illusions to his own work indicated that he was some sort of professor of language or literature. He had a special interest in the idioms of American and English speech.

He wondered how I had found this pub. I told him that an Anglican priest (whom I had met at the conference in Edinburgh) had told me about it, and had said a lot of older gentlemen go there. He laughed and said, *"yes, it was sometimes referred to as 'Jurassic Park.'"* I observed that, in fact, there was quite a mixed age group in the pub.

A lot of those who came in clearly were regulars, greeting various folk as they entered, often with a playful kiss on the cheek. This, however, was not an effeminate crowd. Those who came in were almost all very straight looking and acting. My friend said, *"of course some of the young ones are 'rent boys.'"* I had not heard the term before but did not need to ask its meaning.

There was something about the pub that in the afternoon had the feeling of "The Iceman Cometh." It was a place of palpable loneliness. And there was a kind of sweetness to the camaraderie that men found there. I had the sense that what was most longed for here was not sex but merely connection, touch, embrace - and there was a lot of that. What the Church seems not to see, but would be highly visible here, is the affect of isolating people because of their sexual orientation, so that they grow old without family, outlive their parents, and are sort of the "odd one out" among their siblings. The Church does not want to see this, perhaps because she can think of no way that she would be willing to respond to it.

Though some of them probably do belong to churches, for the most part I think the patrons of this pub have made their departure from organized religion, which has often been organized against them. Most are beyond being angry with the Church, or even too much caring what she does now. As conversations revealed, the Church for many of them has simply become irrelevant. Whatever their religious beliefs or spirituality - and I think it is part of many of these lives - they find and nurture it as best they can on their own. Thinking about the criticism that Jesus suffered for where he hung out and who he hung out with, "*winebibbers and sinners,*" it was easy to imagine Jesus in this pub.

Several years ago, in Columbus, Ohio, for the General Assembly of our church, my friend David Tornblum (see chapter 8), knowing I was working on this book, invited me to go with him to a gay pub called, "The Plugged Nickel," to meet a friend with whom he had corresponded on the Internet. His name was Jeff, and he was seated at the bar when we entered. Jeff is a man probably in his early forties. He manages a gay bowling league (bowling, I learned, is a widely organized sport among many gays), and, being single, he spends many evening hours with friends in this bar. David told him I was writing a book about gay men. Jeff, a very friendly person, immediately said that if I wanted to ask him any questions he'd be glad to answer them. He told me a lot about the gay community in Columbus, which I was surprised to learn is quite large. It wasn't the image I had of Ohio. Columbus, it seems, is not only the state capital but the gay capital of this state.

I asked him if he had a partner. He said he had been in a relationship but it had ended. I inquired if that was something he was looking for. He said he would like that but it hadn't happened. What about persons he met in the bar, I wondered. He was quite emphatic that he had never "tricked" in a bar. The idea of being picked up, or of his picking up someone in this bar, where he spent many hours, to my surprise seemed quite out of the question to him, though I'm sure it was not out of the question to many others in the bar, or in its adjoining night club. It increased my awareness that I had in my own mind too much of a stereotype of the so called "gay life style." What is perhaps most often sought in a gay bar is not sex but friendship, and perhaps a sense of family.

Chapter 12

The Gospel as Song

"Amazing grace, how sweet the sound,
that saved a wretch like me.
I once was lost but now I'm found,
was blind but now I see."

"Amazing Grace." It is perhaps the most universally loved of all hymns; whether played on a banjo, on bagpipes, or by a full symphony orchestra; whether sung in fields of cotton, on a riverbank, or in a great cathedral; whether sung by Mahalia Jackson, Elvis Presley, or Leontyne Price. The words were penned in 1779 by John Newton, who had been, as is well known, a slave trader. His experience of amazing grace was personal, as it is the personal experience of millions.

No two words seem so to capture the experience of all Christians. Dietrich Bonhoeffer speaks of it as "costly grace," grace which "...cost God the life of his son," contrasted to "...that grace which we confer upon ourselves," which he calls, "cheap grace." But there is a grace which in the eyes of some seems to be an abominable grace, a grace that is resented. It is how the grace that the father gives his lost and errant son is seen by his elder brother. This brother, who also received grace, feels cheated, because he believes that his is deserved. Many deny that such grace is given to gays, because they believe it is a grace undeserved. Of course, that's what grace always is - undeserved. If you feel you deserve it, it doesn't feel like grace - nor amazing.

Many believe that grace is drawn from "their" well, and it is off limits to the "unclean" who they think might pollute it.

> *"When Isaac wandered with his clan*
> *into a strange and foreign land,*
> *the locals got up tight about*
>   *their water.*
> *They said, 'The water's ours'*
> *And 'This well is mine, and*
> *frankly we don't like your kind.'*
> *The Lord says, 'I will pour my*
>   *spirit out*
> *on my thirsty sons and daughters.'*
> *So you can keep me from drinking*
>   *from this your well,*
> *But you cannot keep me from*
>   *drinking the water."*
>   from lyrics of
>   "Drinking the Water"
>   by Steve Peterson

My computer has started giving me trouble - again. It freezes on me when I try to get on the web, or retrieve my e-mail. From past experience, I think I know what the problem is. It adds but does not subtract. It stores things in mysterious places and in mysterious ways until the accumulation produces "conflicts" or overloads memory, and the thing freezes on me. My manual typewriter is history, put in some Church rummage sale years ago. My longhand is undecipherable, even by me. Having developed a great dependency on this tool to allow me to do what I want and need to do, I'm now at the mercy of some "tech expert" (probably in India) who I will spend a half hour with me on the phone as he or she helps me "clean it out." As this technician guides me through the dark and subterranean alleyways of my computer, we come upon many programs that are obsolete and unneeded, each designated by an "icon." He or she will have me go here and go there, open this and open that, and drag many of these "icons" to the trash, empty it, and begin again. I'm afraid to try and do this on my own for fear I will trash something essential - something *sacred*. It's intimidating to realize you are an iconoclast, trashing icons.

This is much like a lot of our theology today. We have added without subtracting. We've accumulated doctrine to the point that in the institutional Church we have become, in many ways, dysfunctional. We have one doctrine colliding with another. We ricochet between law and grace trying to please, or appease, what seems like the whimsical will of the Good God/Bad God. We've designated each doctrine as sacred and so feel sacrilegious to "trash" any of them. We associate faith with "holding on" rather than "letting go." In that body we call the Church, we are doctrine-retentive to the point of being somewhat frozen in the normal and healthy functioning of that body. It puts one in mind of the intestinal "blockage" which Martin Luther suffered acutely and which the playwright John Osborne uses in his play, "Young Man Luther," as analogous to Luther's early spiritual condition. The play is based, in part, on Eric Erickson's famous psychoanalytic study of the reformer.

In my interview with the six men, the situation of doctrinal "retentiveness" came up in various ways. John found this "holding on" to be prevalent among those in his college community.

I found it interesting that Westmont had a lot of missionary kids, and preacher's kids, that were raised on this missionary outpost ... by their minister father. They come to this secluded school in the middle of nowhere (Montecito, CA), and have to have a car to get anywhere. There are only 900 students; it's cloistered. I felt sorry for a lot of them because during their whole lives they've been sheltered without questioning anything, and they think they know it all. They think they have their wall built, and they have their gospel verses memorized. Then the first emotional bit that happens in their lives after college and everything falls apart. You have to be able to challenge (yourself), and that isn't going to make you weaker; it's going to make you stronger. And so in a way they are fighting against themselves.

John

I see them as victims. They are held by a fear that has been constructed for them. And you talk to them... about the sins of the fathers being visited on the children to the third and fourth generation...and of not believing exactly what we've been taught. And you start questioning, and you wonder what else have I been taught that may not be true. "My God, I've got to start thinking!" And that's a very scary thing, rather than have a little model of how we live, and how God operates, and everything else, rather than saying, "there is the Bible and all the answers are right there." So they keep the fear, and people don't want to let go of that fear, because there's a certain comfort in having everything explained for you.

Neal

What's surprising is that the world does not fall apart, and that God is not going to disappear.

John

There is some doctrine we need to drag to the trash, and we haven't the courage to do it. We seem to be a afraid that our theology is a delicate house of cards and if we remove one (i.e. the virgin birth, or the bodily resurrection) the whole structure will collapse.

I think there is a bigger fear. I call it the slippery-slope theory. The fear is that people, particularly in religious communities, and people that believe that the Bible stories tell them that homosexuality is wrong, fear that if (their) belief about that is wrong then what are our other religious beliefs that are wrong? And we can go through a whole list of fears; "maybe Jesus didn't die for me, or maybe Jesus wasn't God." The ultimate fear is, "maybe God doesn't exist, and therefore I am lost." That is the ultimate fear and so a big wall is built up. The fear is that eventually the whole wall will crumble and they will be lost.
Neal

That fear is not because of faith but because of the lack of it. Fundamentalist preachers often provoke just that fear among their followers and among themselves. Unless you see it - all of it - just their way, there is no salvation. Question any of it, they believe, and there will be nothing left, nothing to hang onto. But many gay men and women have had to do that to survive psychologically and spiritually. They have had to drag a lot of what they have been taught, or has been imposed on them theologically, to the trash so that what is essential could remain. Therefore, many of these are, even if unintentionally, pioneers who push out a new theological frontier for the Church. Being survivors, they have also discovered that God is sturdier than is generally thought, and is not of such fragile ego and volatile temperament that he/she cannot bear the asking of real questions.

Jesus is taught as being a very mystical kind of person and I always thought of him more as an action figure, radical, but still very mysterious. I don't claim to have Jesus figured out, and his combination with God, so I'll go back to what the nuns told us. If you couldn't come up with an answer, they would always say, "It's a mystery." God has changed (in my experience) since my conversion, and my coming out and being comfortable with my sexuality. I feel not only that I have been liberated, but that God has been liberated.

We've been talking about the Bible as this rule book, and that there are answers to everything there. I don't think that so much as that it is a tool to help us understand our lives. And (it) has been used as a tool to try to keep God inside a fence, or a box, and everything is contained. You know all about God and try to keep God in a box. So many things I've been taught I know now aren't right, so that I can let God out of the box, and God can be God and God can do whatever God wants to do.

You can't say the word "can't" with God. God loves us, and if God provides us with something else (other than we expect), that's fine. I'm no longer in need of a structured universe with God on top, where everything goes around in perfect harmony, (so that) if we believe something different it spins the whole thing into chaos. If God wants to mess around, then fine, just grab hold and go for the ride and shout "whoopee!" You're going to have a lot better time than trying to keep God, and your life, and everybody else, in a box."

Neal

Along the same lines when I was at BIOLA (Bible Institute of Los Angeles) we had a professor on Revelations - but he called it New Testament - who at the beginning of the class polled the entire class to find out how many were premillennial and how many were a-millennial. He polled the class to see how many converts he would have, and he was really into it. There were four of us who were fraternity members and we decided to play with him, and when he took the end of the course poll he was four shy which, of course, threw his little survey into chaos, and he demanded to know who the four were that didn't vote. And we stood up and identified ourselves - as pro-millennial. And he said, "What is pro-millennial?" And we said, "Whatever God decides we're in favor of it."

And that really was an experience for me because for the first time (I knew), "Yeah, that's sort of the way it works. It really is whatever God decides, that's the way it is. The fact that I'm gay, that's the way it is." We can take our polls, we can do churchy things, but the truth is God does have the last say. It was a very good experience for me.

Paul

In America's own story of opening the frontier many of those who first went West did so out of a drive for adventure or a lust for gold. But many went West not because they were extraordinarily visionary or brave, but because they were leaving behind a life that just was not working for them where they were; or they left because there was nothing there to really hold them back. Perhaps that was true even for Abram when he left Ur. Many gay and lesbian persons have gone before us, taking the risks we will not take, because hope has been only before them not in backward glances. They could not go back. They could only go forward or die - if not physically, then spiritually.

The Church, if she were wise, would eagerly embrace them, not to prove her generosity but because she needs them. Many gay, lesbian, bisexual, and transgender persons have been compelled to discover, and many more are now discovering, that they do not need the institutional

Church to have God in their lives. If the Church continues to denigrate them and their relationships, to be self-affirming and life-affirming they must leave it even if they are greatly reluctant to go from that which at one time was deeply meaningful to them. They've learned that the experience of God is not altogether one with others' ideas about the nature of God. Nonetheless, for many of these persons there remains a nostalgia about the Church as a community which, for all of its faults, led them toward an experience of God.

That nostalgia was very evident on the evening a couple of years ago that I spent in the piano bar at Gentry's in Chicago and heard Job Christianson sing, "His Eye is on the Sparrow."

"I sing because I'm happy.
I sing because I'm free.
For his eye is on the sparrow,
and I know He watches me."

He had touched upon their spiritual hunger. How has the Church, much of it at least, responded to that hunger? Gay men and women have asked for bread and have been given a stone. The Church has given them answers without even knowing the real questions. Not allowing the asking of a question to which she does not have a predetermined answer, the Church's answers have been to her own questions, not to those of gay and lesbian persons. Love, truth, compassion and peace, seem meager now, and wholly politicized in the ecclesiastical wars.

What statements can we make about God and Jesus Christ that are descriptive of our experience, faithful to scripture as a unique and authoritative witness, but while using scripture as guidance are not in bondage to old doctrinal formulations and images? First, if we concede, based on scripture itself, that God's self revelation in history is progressive from Abraham to the New Testament authors, we have reason to believe that this revelation does not close with the New Testament. Scripture itself alludes to God going before us. No one generation, including our own, dare claim that revelation, as they see it or understand it, is complete for every age and for every individual.

Back in the 60's when the orthodoxy of Episcopal Bishop James Pike was being challenged, he was asked if in good conscience he could say the creed (presumably the Apostles' or Nicene Creed), and he answered that he could not say it - but he could *sing it*. In the experience of many, there is not much in our theology that sings anymore. Our rigid orthodoxy is cold and leaden, armor-plated, against any unwelcome intrusion of the Spirit.

I sometimes lay awake at night now wondering how long I can stay in an institution that I know is the enemy, as William Stringfellow's book in the 1960's ("My People is the Enemy") was titled. Where other persons and institutions are abusive, they look to the Church for their justification to act as they do, and appalling as it may be to the Church, many believe they find it there.

Perhaps more than anything else the music of the Church binds me to her. Sometimes it is only the music that makes it bearable. And the music is as diverse as the Church itself, and I seem to love most all of it: the great old Gospel hymns, the grand Reformation hymns, Handle, Beethoven, Bach, plainsong and chants; and also folk, the Caribbean rhythms, country, jazz, "Jesus Christ Superstar," and "Godspell." But recently something was added to my experience - Morticia DeVille and the Gospel Echoes. Morticia is a large bewigged and glittered drag queen who sings in a big voice, flanked on either side by the Gospel Echoes, two young men with fine voices. Mostly they sing songs about getting to heaven, and coming from Morticia's large voice and larger persona, it has implicit attitude..."*you may as well love us now honey, cause we will be there*." This is serious, not put on. They have been singing gospel for nearly 16 years in a gay bar in Atlanta.

Speaking of the hereafter, I've no real idea what it may be like, but it makes me think of something once said by Albert Einstein's wife when she was asked if she understood her husband's theory of relativity. She responded, *"No, but I know Albert, and I know he can be trusted."*

My trust is not in knowing what the hereafter may be like, but my trust is in the One who will lead me there. It isn't every moment of my life, but there are moments, and most of all perhaps moments when I am in the midst of God's people singing, that I know in whom I have believed, and I know that that One can be trusted. Music puts wings to our theologizing. Music gives heart to what might be our cold rationalism. Music takes some of the fear out of unknowing. And the church has always sung.

There's a little statement in Matthew that tends to slip by our consciousness, but it tells us something very important. On the evening of the last supper, it says that before they left that upper room, *"...after singing the Passover hymn they went out to the Mount of Olives."* They sang! Now, there is a picture for your mind. Think of those men in Leonardo de Vinci's "Last Supper," before they go out, singing.

One evening, several years ago, my wife and I were surfing our TV channels, searching for something we would feel at all inclined to watch. We came upon a kind of sing-along - in promotion of a newly released album produced by Bill Gaither - of the music of the Billy Graham crusades. There was Mrs Graham, George Beverly Shea, and Cliff Barrows, who like myself had strangely grown much older (Billy was ill and could not be present). There were about twenty persons seated around the piano, many of whom at one time or another had been soloists with the Crusade. Shea sang, "How Great Thou Art." His voice is not what it was on the many evenings that I heard him sing in the Old

Madison Square Garden during Graham's 1956 Crusade; still it moved me to hear it.

As we listened, sadness fell over me, and with it anger. I recalled when the Gospel was preached to fill hearts and to heal broken ones. Listening to those hymns, I felt overwhelming sadness that others, lusting power and influence and sometimes wealth and celebrity, had turned the Gospel into something crass, harsh and divisive.

My own vision of the Church has been to think of her as a great orchestra. God is the maestro, Jesus the first violist to whom the whole orchestra tunes. He, though the first violist might be a she, is the "prince" of the orchestra - on the maestro's *left* hand as he (or she) conducts. Under this imagery, "sin" is more rightly understood not as "bad deeds," but of being off pitch, off time, which is very much like the meaning of the Greek word for sin (hammartia) which is "to miss the mark."

And what is the music? Some will rush to say that it is scripture, the word of God written, but we should remember that music itself is not something written, though it may be referred to that way. What is written down is a guide to music, and it may have been written down centuries ago. But music itself is not for the eye, but for the ear. Music exists in the hearing, first in the mind of the composer/creator, and then the one who plays it, the evangelist, and finally in the ear of the hearer. Not scripture, but The Word going forth from the mind of God to the ear of the hearer, is the music. It goes forth on the wind, on breath, on the waves of the air - the Holy Spirit. *"Those who have ears to hear let them hear"* - the music.

Thinking of the Church as orchestra, consider its diversity. Remember what we learned about the orchestra from "Peter and the Wolf?" There are four main sections; the strings, woodwinds, brass, and percussion. And within them there is much diversity. The strings consist of violins, and violas, cellos, bass, and harp. The piano (which is also a percussion instrument) is a stringed instrument. For a particular composition the strings might also include the guitar. The woodwinds consist of various clarinets, of flutes, and oboes. The brass includes trumpets, coronets, saxophones, french horns, trombones, tubas, and the bass horn. The percussion, besides various drums including the timpani, also includes cymbals, bells, chimes, perhaps a xylophone, castanets, and any variety of other sound producing instruments struck by hand, stick, hammer, brush, or each other. For Tchaikousky's "1812 Overture," percussion might also include a canon.

What of these instruments shall we call profane, alien, unworthy, an abomination, and drive out of the orchestra, or demand they never be sounded? How would the music change to leave out the strange looking oboe, the cumbersome bass, the insinuating sound of the flute, or the thundering timpani? Should the maestro have his or her way, or should each musician play as he or she feels they would like to? Doesn't the sovereignty of God mean precisely that the conductor decides and guides? The conductor conducts and the orchestra follows doing the maestro's will, so that the music goes forth from the mind of the conductor to the ear of the hearer.

What irony it is that so much of the music that has put wings under of our fragile, frightened faith, has come from gay organists, choir directors, singers, and composers.

For the Church to exclude gays is to exclude their religious experience, which is to exclude the Christ who has "appeared" to them out of the painful experiences of their lives. If we push gays in the closet, Jesus goes with them, not with us. We are rejecting witnesses who have journeyed where we have not, and the resurrected Christ has walked with them on that road and appeared to them in the breaking of the bread we have withheld. We cannot set the rules of Christ's acceptance of them, for Christ is free to accept whomever He will, and we are merely the witnesses.

I think we're in a community where we have a complete spectrum from one end to the other about the nature of God. In that sense what I focus on is the journey of the believer, so that at any one point in time you might ask me what my thoughts are, and I'll at least at that point in time decide I can think about it a little bit more and give an answer.

Gerald

In Bethlehem, God made a largely unwelcome intrusion into the world so that a child might grow among others *"full of grace and truth,"* and so that, as a man, his life, death, and resurrection would make a dead orthodoxy sing. Jesus comes as the logos of God - "the Word" - set in the world as model of "what God is like." Jesus is God *in the world*, - those are the lyrics, the Christ is God *within us*, that is the song. Christ comes to us in others. Christ goes to others through us. Christ comes to us in the one who sees us (as Jesus saw Zaccaheus up a tree), hears us, knows us, loves us, heals us, restores us, resurrects and saves us. Christ is present to us in others including gay men and women.

The most remarkable thing about the "appearances" of Jesus after the resurrection is that no one (Mary, the men on the Emmaus Road, Thomas, the fishermen in Galilee) sees him and exclaims, *"There's Jesus! It's him! I recognize that familiar face of the man I knew so well!"* That most expected kind of recognition doesn't happen or is never mentioned if it did. He is recognized in speaking Mary's name, in the breaking of bread, in Thomas's touching of his wounds, in the hauling-in of fish.

The witnesses do not attest to knowing the resurrected Christ by his appearance, the way we recognize others. He is recognized in his addressing their fears, their longing, their doubt, and their despair. And he comes to us and we recognize him in very personal experience, in intimate signs: the way he speaks our name, in the bread broken for us, in his touching of our wounds, in a bountiful and rebirthing dawn after a dreary night of hauling in empty nets in our dark dreams.

Isn't it curious that the person who is the center of the whole New Testament is never physically described in any way? There is no mention of whether he was tall or short, dark or light skinned, the color of his eyes, the cut of his jaw, whether his hair was thick or thin, curly or straight. There is nothing about his smile, or laughter, nothing about whether his nose was straight or somewhat curved, nothing about the size of his hands or feet, or his general build. The imprint of the crucified Christ on the shroud of Turin, the authenticity of which may be forever in doubt, is as close as we get. Yet probably no body has been more often painted or rendered in stone and marble, wood and clay than this body. Artists have been given total freedom to see him with their own eyes, and in their own imaginations, and through their own experience. It is a freedom given to every believer. I cannot but believe that this "great omission" by the authors of the gospels is other than intentional and providential. It is how the resurrected Christ still comes to us. It is how He comes to gay men, among others, and no one has the right to deny what they have seen and heard and known.

Just as no one owns the physical image of Jesus, so no one owns the Gospel itself. When scriptures are quoted "at" gays, it is often forgotten that it is their Bible, too. Also the invitation of the Church is not the members; but Christ's invitation. The sacraments are for gays who receive them with open hearts; it is not "our" table but the

Lord's table. And the gifts God gives them and the ministry to which God calls them is theirs, despite whoever refuses to validate that. The prayers, the confessions, and the songs are theirs. The institutional Church may try to privatize the Gospel, and deny them the fellowship, the sacraments, and the ministry. But that is only the visible Church. As the artist conjures an image of Jesus in his or her mind, good as it may be, it is not itself the face of Jesus. If various believers conjure a Church in their minds, good as it may be, it is not itself the body of Christ.

On the last evening of the international conference I attended in Edinburgh, they had a Ceilidh (Scottish dancing) and I saw the children of God dancing. A few at first, and slowly, then the many: men, women, straight, gay, men and women, men with men, and women with women, English, Scott, Irish, French, German, Swiss, Italian, Scandinavian, Dutch, dancing - swinging each other in a wild reel, arm to arm, body to body, joining hands, joining hearts, Protestant, Catholic, young and old, graceful and not so graceful. I was dancing too. It was the purest image of the Family of God I thought I had ever seen. I thought that for a few minutes I was seeing us as God sees us, as children, and felt some of the tenderness of God toward us. It is one of those moments when nothing is spoken but everything is known - in the heart. After a while, the dancing ended, they sang *"Auld Lang Syne"* and began drifting away, exhausted by joy.

It is this picture, this experience of wholeness, of holiness, that is the very meaning of shalom.

Chapter 13

Coming In

Joe asks his friend Will, who is African American - and
 gay: "Is it harder in our society to be black or to be gay?
With only a moment's hesitation Will replies: "It's harder
 to be gay."
Joe: *"Why is that?"*
Will: *"Because man, if you're black, you don't have to tell
 your parents."*

There is for gay and lesbian persons one more rite of passage than is likely to exist in the lives of others, and it may be the single most life changing passage they will go through. It is their coming out. Debutantes used to "come out," but not homosexuals. Forty years ago "coming out" was a fairly novel concept - and hazardous. Persons were either exposed, or the object of rumor, or deeply closeted, or they went away to some place of relative anonymity, where they could sometimes, privately and/or secretly, be themselves. It is not easy to conceive of the fear and shame attached to this for many persons who struggle to come out even to themselves.

A friend of mine died recently. He was in his early 80's. He and his partner had lived together in a close and loving relationship for 48 years. Most of their relatives had passed on. They were retired for many years. All the reasons why many are fearful of coming out of the closet no longer really existed for them. Yet my friend who died, in many situations, was still reluctant to let on that he was really gay and that his partner was in fact the love of his life. If someone wanted to know if he was gay, he would simply say, "*I am a human being.*" The imprint of shame, going back nearly a half century, still lingered in him. Part of what attested to the love between them was that his partner, comfortable with his own sexuality, did not share that anxiety though he understood it, and always respected his partner's need to be somewhat closeted. Coming out is often a fearful thing. Some persons never come out; they die in the closet.

So why do it? Straight people don't "come out?" They don't talk about their sexuality. They don't name their proclivities. Well, actually in certain contexts some do, women over coffee perhaps, men over beer. But certainly not in the Church. Well, straight people don't have to. No one is challenging their right to be themselves. Others may criticize some of the behavior of straight persons, but not their nature. Sometimes persons will tell me that their objection to persons "coming out" is that sex is personal, private, and does not need to be talked about. Most gay persons feel their sexual lives are personal and private, and would like them treated that way. However, there is a substantial difference between a private life and life in the closet. Coming out is made necessary because of the many who speculate and make judgments about the lives and relationships of others as a basis for their intolerance, discrimination, and general mistreatment - if not open abuse - of them. Gays come out because only by coming out can they be empowered to act in their own self-interest and defense. You cannot fight injustice by acquiescence to being treated unjustly, or from a place where you are made invisible and silent.

The first coming out of gay persons is to themselves. For some, that happens very early, but for many, that coming out to themselves is traumatic on its own. For some, the cost of such self acknowledgement may even be life threatening. Some gays have not come out to themselves until they are in their late twenties or in their thirties, and some later than that.

Coming out to others poses various levels of concern for individuals. There are issues of the effect that such revelation may have on others, especially family members. The younger generation, by and large, will probably have less difficulty because precedents will have been set for them, and because general social tolerance has grown - though not so much in the Church. Persons will tend to be open to themselves sooner, and will be less likely to foreclose on various options for their lives.

John came out to his mother on her birthday:

I took my mom out for her birthday, and decided that was a good time to tell her that I was gay. We went to "Fiddler on the Roof" that night and this whole thing happened because of this idea about "roles" (traditional masculine and feminine roles). She came to the apartment and there was a huge bouquet of flowers there. She said, "What are those?"

"They're flowers."
"Why do you have them on your desk?"
'Well, someone gave them to me."
"Well, who gave them to you?"
"Neal did."
"Well, why would a guy give another guy flowers?"
"Well, mom, I'm kind of dating him."
And her response was, "Well, who wears the high heels?"
"Excuse me?" I said, "If I'd wanted to go with a woman I'd be with a woman. But, I'm not, I'm going with Neal."
That was her birthday present, and at the intermission we're out there at The Dorothy Chandler and she's crying and looking at me like I'd just punched her.
"I don't understand it, it can't be happening."

"Well, it is," I said, and we went back in.
After the show we get in the car and we're going back to the apartment and she said,
 "Well, what are you doing tonight?"
 "I'm going to have dinner with Neal."
And she said, "Can I come and have dinner with you?"
And we got back to the apartment and I called Neal and said, "Guess who's coming to dinner?"

In the years that Neal and I have been together I've found it very freeing that we don't have these ideas of fixed roles. If I want to cook, or bake cookies, or whatever - or if Neal does - it doesn't matter. If he wants to go out there and clean up the dog poop or mow the lawn, I don't care. We don't have that feeling that one has to be one thing and one has to be the other. It's extremely freeing when you're not riveted to "you can only cook or sew, or you can only work on cars."

In Mark Thompson's "Gay Soul," part of a trilogy on Gay Soul, Mind, and Body, someone speaks of there being a "coming out" and a "coming in." Part of the stories that I hear from the gay men that I know is of their "coming in" after a long journey through turbulent times and over rough terrain.

I even got married trying to prove a point to somebody. I could not live another day feeling like an abomination. I finally said, "If I'm an abomination in your eyes then, God, I want nothing to do with you. Get out of my life!" And it was many, many years before I came anywhere near any sense or desire to come back (to a) church, because I felt there was nothing there for me. I felt like I was the orphan that got kicked out of the house and had to go live on the street, and I said, "I'll prove I can live on the street and survive," and I felt a sense of pride in a way that I didn't depend on the Church. The Church didn't have anything to do with me...The people in the Church, the ones I knew, were the ones that were being kicked around, letting the minister tell them what they ought to think. I was kind of pleased to be out of it for the longest time, and it was a very long journey back."

If someone, when you're small teaches you that you're a freak, so you hate your own guts...,well, for me it's been a long process undoing that. I will think it's undone and something happens and I go, "Oh, there's another layer of it to get rid of."

David

....Sooner or later other people came along with different voices that had more a message of love and acceptance, and (encouragement) to get rid of the fear and so forth. And it made a lot more sense. It wasn't that I went to look for a particular Christian study to contradict the other stuff, it was just coming into touch with people who were not fearful, who seemed to be joyous and able to alleviate (other's) fears with their explanation of what the Gospel was and who God was....a God of love and encouragement and unlimited forgiveness. Everything wasn't driven by fear, and it was nice to have that fear gone. That transition (in me) came from their lives.

Neal

Neal talks about God loving us, always, unconditionally, and that love won't change. What is most significant in that is not in its being any sort of original theological proposition, it is a statement many Christians, conservative and liberal, might make, though with some it is given with one hand and taken back with the other. Its significance is that it comes for him and other gay Christians after a journey and it's not as a crib note for personal evangelism, nor as an intellectual conviction from theological reflection, but as knowledge engraved on the heart from personal experience.

One of the radio talk show commentators snickered at homosexuals calling themselves "gay." He said it is just the opposite, *"...look at the promiscuity, AIDS, broken relationships, alcoholism, and suicide."* There is a lot in being gay that is difficult, painful and sometimes dark; and much of that is the direct result of how society treats them. Nonetheless, even if paradoxical, the term "gay" is often remarkably fitting. As has been said by others, when you have done the worst that you can do toward others and they survive, they win. They are the ones then who are liberated, and yes, gay. They often have humor, and grace, and creativity, attributes they have cultivated that have helped them survive.

I remember having this epiphany. I was living in New York City, and I was walking down Columbus Avenue, sort of mindlessly window-shopping. I wasn't thinking any particularly deep thoughts, when suddenly, out of nowhere, I had this realization that everything good about my life had sprung from the fact that I was gay. Everything had its root in that. Because I was gay, I had been forced to think differently than the people around me. I had been forced to get an education so I could leave this small town my family lived in. Because I was gay, I had become good at being a chameleon and fitting in places, so as a result I had become a very intuitive and creative person. Being gay had forced me to learn and grow in order to survive. It had given me courage, passion, commitment, resolve, a sense of justice, my sense of humor, my compassion for others - particularly the 'different' people of the world.

Basically everything that brought me joy or pride was the result of my having been born a gay man. It was like my life was this ladder, and for the first time I could see how each step had brought me closer to the man I'd become. Every bad and painful thing had just been a portal - a doorway to something better. And in that moment, I felt so completely grateful to be gay. I was so pleased with it. What a wonderful thing this had turned out to be. It was the beginning of my feeling genuinely good about myself. I felt so strong. I had found this image of myself that no one could scratch or mar. It didn't matter now how many scriptures were quoted at me. If fifteen teenage boys had driven by at that moment and screamed 'faggot!' out their car window, it wouldn't have touched me. I had found this core truth - this way of loving myself, and no one could ever take that from me again.

David

Many people think "gay" is a misnomer, but in so many instances it is exactly right. In their coming in they who could not rely on the welcome of others, have created their own community and their own welcome. They have learned to love and care for each other in extraordinary ways. Oppression has bonded them (especially AIDS), and it is a remarkable thing to behold. The evil that has been done to them they have turned into a gift.

*"The chains they used to bind us
have been changed to fearless pride.
And the words they used to maim us
have become our battle cry.
And we will not give up hope until
the last one is set free,
and we can sing,
let freedom ring!"*
from a song by Steve Peterson

Their coming in has meant for many of them a coming back to their faith, even if not to their faith communities, from which they were effectively driven out and sent elsewhere. They have found the elsewhere and turned it into a home.

I asked the men I interviewed if they could identify a moment in their lives when their religious orientation and their sexual orientation collided.

I went to L.A. and I met up with a friend of mine named Bob. Bob was the guy who led all our Bible studies at school. He was the spiritual leader of our dorm. I ran into him and he looked completely different. He went to the gym and had this incredible hard body and before he was not at all like that. He had a friend named Craig, and Craig was looking for someone to share an apartment. So, we ended up being roommates. Bob came down one night to have dinner with us - and here we go again!
He said, "I have something to tell you."
"What is it?"
And he said, "I'm gay."
And I said, "What's happening here? all of my friends are coming out!"
And I said, "You're a Christian you can't be gay."
And he said, "No, you can"
And I went, "Oh my goodness I don't understand it."
So we finished dinner and Craig said we didn't have any dessert, and asked me to go to Ralph's and get some ice cream. So, true to form, I left and didn't come back. I went to get ice cream and didn't come back that night, because I couldn't face it. But this time I decided I wasn't going to let it go. I called Bob and he said he was leading a Bible study, a gay Bible study. I went to the Bible study and that's where I met Neal. We started dating and we've been together ever since.   John

In my experience, I think there were two major collisions. First, I was studying to be a minister, and also I was fighting my sexuality. I was in college and had realized I was gay and was in complete denial and wanted to do anything I could to get rid of that "phase," that part of my life, and truly believing all that balderdash about, "You'd better pray for your life and whatever you pray for will happen." So after years of praying...I realized it was not going to change, and I tried just about everything, and eventually decided that I would come out to my parents. ....I eventually ended up with a Christian psychiatrist, which means you add the word "Christian" on a calling card. And that did not work, and after almost a year of therapy, I attempted suicide and that was my way out. Upon recovering from that, and some psychotherapy with a counselor who said gay was O.K., I had a better grasp on things. My first counselor (had) said it wasn't compatible and get out. I quit going to church altogether and moved to Las Vegas. The second collision was that I still had the need in my life and hadn't come to grips with that, and I was reading 'The Advocate' one Saturday night and saw a small ad for WHPC (West Hollywood Presbyterian Church), and the catch phrase for it was: "...for those who felt they didn't like the 'church.'" My problem was I loved church, that's where I thought I belonged, but I felt the Church didn't like me. So the second collision was very favorable in that for once I was able to go and discover the possibility of being gay and Christian, and that was an amazing transformation for me, and that was 22 years ago. And just walking into the courtyard of WHPC, I was greeted by Ross (Ross Greek, former pastor). And naturally, me being a good Christian, I wore a three piece suit. I was immediately greeted by people in jeans and shorts. And Ross Greek looked at me and decided this could be one who was wondering what was going on here; and he pulled me aside as we were going in and said, "I want you to know you're going to meet people inside who are gay." And for the first time in my life I was able to identify myself as gay. It was the first time, other than therapy, I had actually used the word gay and had any sense of pride in it. So that was an amazing collision on a positive note. The first one being kind of tragic and the second one finding a whole new life.

Paul

My collision was in college and it was also positive. It was at a Christian college and we all had religion as a minor. But I really enjoyed all that and I liked the experience of hanging out with some of the more radical/liberal professors. I was increasingly aware that I was gay. I remember praying one night that God would take it away from me. "Release me! Release me from all of that!" And I was praying for that and I had a conversation with God and in essence God said to me, "Now wait a minute, have I ever withheld anything from you, or given anything but the best for you? Have I ever not loved you? Have I ever rejected you?" And all I could say was, "No God." And God said, "If I haven't rejected you then who are you to reject yourself?" And that kind of hit me, and it was something I had to think about for quite a while. Also, going downtown to Chicago, there was a bookstore with magazines like "The Advocate," and a Broadway magazine called "After Dark," that was gay as could be. And I remember looking in "The Advocate," in the black and white little ads, and the personal ads, and trying to figure out what some of the codes meant, and there was one that said, "Christian and gay?" And I wrote in for a free booklet, by Dr. Ralph Blair, and it was a wonderful booklet that went through all the spiritual (Biblical) passages from a different stand-point, and this was something we were trained to do...and "Oh, my God, the author got it right and it's completely different and opposite of what was in our

Bible courses, and everyone else is saying." I was walking around thinking, "I've got a secret - you've got it all wrong!" The combination of those two things: one very personal, and one intellectual, was very powerful.

Neal

An opportunity arose for me to come to L.A., and so I did that and tried to sort out my sexual experience from my spiritual. What happened was that after I got here, I determined that because of my physical desire, my intellectual and spiritual life were not connected with my physical being. I couldn't handle it. It was a crisis. I decided there was something really wrong. I don't know how but I knew where the gay bars were, and I decided that was what I was going to do...I was going to go there and I didn't care if God wanted me to go there or not.

That's how I had my crisis point. It was all planned. It was Feb. 14, 1975, I went into that gay world. I never gave up my other straight community at all, and I had dual communities - typical closet thing. At some point Ross Greek was there for me too. I was doing the dual thing but for the first time I had feeling. I was doing all these outrageous things, acting on my gay identity, but I found another gay community at West Hollywood Presbyterian Church. I was in a euphoric state for weeks at a time, and not feeling guilt. A gay bar was a hard place to go. In my tradition there was no drinking, no dancing, and no smoking; in the gay bar they were doing all three at the same time.

Gerald

The church these men came back to was an extraordinary church in the sense that it has a predominantly gay membership. It was easier to feel the welcome and the inclusion there. There are now many churches that regard themselves as open, as welcoming and affirming of gays as of all others. Some have made an open declaration of that and are perhaps willing to ordain them and validate them in leadership roles within the Church, to celebrate their "holy unions," and to advocate for their rights within the church and in the wider society. That takes some courage, and presently it costs them something, because it is sometimes an act of ecclesiastical disobedience. Hopefully, there are gays who had given up on the church who will find these churches and receive their welcome.

There are also a great many congregations who feel there is no problem if gays come into their church - quietly, *as though nothing has happened.* But something has happened! Something terribly significant for gays. More than mere inclusion is needed. There needs to be reconciliation. How does that happen? Gays themselves do not usually want some conspicuous action focused on their sexual orientation, any more than a straight person would. But painful history and alienation need to be acknowledged in order to move into a new relationship. The Church that truly has the heart and the desire to do that will find the way. But simply to pretend it never happened, that no injury occurred, is not the way.

Any form of peace and reconciliation that allows the sin of injustice and oppression to continue is a false peace and a counterfeit reconciliation. This kind of "reconciliation" has nothing whatsoever to do with the Christian faith....What this means in practice is that no reconciliation, no forgiveness and no negotiations are possible without repentance."
The Kairos Document, Challenge to the Church: A Theological Comment on the Political Crisis in South Africa, Revised Second Edition 1986

The West Hollywood Presbyterian Church and other welcoming churches are made up of those who may have been counseled in one church to "go somewhere else where they would probably be happier." And, of course, faced with such unwelcome, they do go away, but it is the Church which is the loser. Sometimes a person will ask, "Well, what if we welcome them and they all come here?" I've heard that question asked of Rev. Peg Beissert, my predecessor as Director of The Lazarus Project, and she will throw her arms in the air and say, *"You should be so lucky!"*

It won't happen. Gays have learned, if they approach the Church at all, they do so warily. Even when our churches may formally welcome gays into their life, there is a long journey ahead for gays to trust the Church again.

Gays take care of each other in remarkable ways. And they are tough. Although it may not have been their nature to be that way, they were made tough by surviving the taunters and the schoolyard bullies. Many gays remember high school as simply an ordeal to get through. One gay friend, now a college math professor, said he got through high school *"cleverly disguised as a nerd."*

For the city dwellers in Jerusalem, Nazareth and Galilee were Appalachia, that is, they were rural - not the city, nor the suburb, not Jerusalem nor Bethany nor Bethlehem. In what is called the Sermon On The Mount, what Jesus says tells you something about who he was talking to: the meek, those who mourn, the non-aggressive, those reviled and persecuted. What is the meaning of meek? The meaning is not - weak? Gays are often the meek, but they are not often the weak. The battle enjoined with many Christian fundamentalists is an odd one in that it pits the meek against bullies. Their bullying is to cover fears they cannot acknowledge and probably do not understand.

++++

Sometimes it is hard to put our picture of Jesus together, which is no doubt why so many perceive him in so many different ways. In many passages we see him as one of infinite compassion and mercy, and it leaves us unprepared for moments when He speaks with a directness, and even it seems a heartlessness, that startles us. Such a moment is in the eighth chapter of Matthew which gives an account of the calling of some of his disciples; *"....one of his disciples, said to him, 'Lord, let me go and bury my father first,' Jesus replied, 'Follow me, and leave the dead to bury their dead.'"* (Matthew 8:21-22) It is this invitation, this exhortation, that the Church is loathe to hear. They are willing enough to follow if only it doesn't entail leaving, or leaving before "the way be clear." It is an extraordinary call that comes to us. There is in the Gospels this relentless sense of urgency about the mission. It cannot be put off. *"Do it now!"* is Jesus' message. And toward the disciple in this passage it seems heartless. Does it mean Jesus will not give him another day (as was the custom) in which to bury his father? And what about the commandment to *"honor thy father and mother?"* Should he not have some time to mourn - time in which to honor his father, and time to comfort his mother and to see that she will be taken care of? But perhaps such literalness misses the point. The man's father may not have just died. Maybe the disciple means: *"I'd like to follow now, but I can't do that while my father is still alive. We have a family business here. He counts on me. If I leave now it will be without his blessing. I may be cut off from my inheritance. But when I can - I will."*

Isn't that good enough? Shouldn't it be? Not if we hear Jesus' call to follow - now. Or is the message here that we are to move on from what is past and dead, to do the living thing? Shall our fathers hold us back? Is this about a literal burial, or is it about priorities, about the courage to leave the dead past and take up this dangerous mission? Shall we not move until those who are dead (not in the physical sense - but dead to this new thing) are buried? Shall we not challenge our congregations to respond to Christ's call though they have heard it, until those who hold to the past, to what is dead, are gone and with them, their objections? The sense of urgency that is present in this passage seems rarely to be present in obeying the call when it comes to gay and lesbian persons. The message always goes out that first we must take care of those who are dead to this Word.

There's an old gospel hymn that goes:
"Farther along we'll know all about it.
Farther along we'll understand why.
Cheer up, my brothers, live in the sunlight.
We'll understand it all bye and bye."

Gays in our society today know they are not where they have been. They also know that with a certain inevitability they are not yet where they will be - farther along. They are living in the "meanwhile," but are not living there passively, simply waiting for the wider society to get around to making this a just and inclusive society. Meanwhile though, much of the depression has lifted, and they have chosen to live in the sunlight, even now. That's why the term "gay" fits.

To know gay and lesbian persons will be to know ourselves better. To understand gay and lesbian persons will be to understand ourselves more completely. To love gay and lesbian persons will be to love ourselves more deeply. Even a true desire to understand them rather than judge them would bring us halfway there. But what one so often encounters in others is a resistance to knowing them, a refusal to understand them, and a pretense to love them.

When we exclude gay persons, (and despite artful

language that is what we have been doing), we exclude something of The Word itself. We distort the Word because we have already closed our ears to it, as though we excluded a theme within a symphonic work, or as though we excluded one note in an octave as an unfit note. The Church then can only make a discordant sound.

When the prodigal son came home, the father didn't just say, *"Welcome home, son. I've laid out some fresh towels in the bath for you. Rest up and then come down for super."* And meanwhile he tries to think how to ward off the older son's anger when he comes home and finds his younger brother there. That's not the story. The story is the father saw his lost son from afar off and ran out to him, and gathered him in his arms, kissed him, and put a fine robe on him and a ring on his finger. He restored the lad's dignity, and threw a party to celebrate his homecoming. The returning son also has his part to do, dealing with some deep and heartfelt regret for the mess he has made of his life. That's reconciliation! But with the older brother, reconciliation does not come easily, if at all. When he comes home, he is outraged at his father's lavish welcome of his brother. His father's grace toward his younger son is to the older brother an *abominable grace*. The father addresses his oldest son's anger and is straightforward about his feelings for both of his sons. The story ends there. We are not told what happens over time between the two brothers. Are they reconciled? Perhaps Jesus leaves it for us to write this ending. How will we write it in relation to our gay brother and sister?

There is another story of brothers in scripture which perhaps offers us some insight into the meaning of reconciliation:

And Jacob was left alone; and a man wrestled with him until the breaking of day. When the man saw that he did not prevail against Jacob, he touched the hollow of his thigh; and Jacob's thigh was put out of joint as he wrestled with him. Then he said, "Let me go, for the day is breaking." But Jacob said, "I will not let you go, unless you bless me." And he said, "What is your name?" And he said, "Jacob." Then he said, "You're name shall no more be called Jacob, but Israel, for you have striven with God and with men, and have prevailed."
Genesis 32:24-28

A Bible professor of mine once began a lecture about Jacob saying, *"Now here we have a man so crooked he had to screw his socks on."* Yet God used him, making him the father of all the tribes of Israel. But first God had to change this opportunist. That change came, signified in his being given a new name, in the night before, after years of estrangement, he was to be face to face with his twin brother from whom he had stolen the birthright. Fearful of what the next day would bring, through the night, a man, it says, wrestled with him. Though it seems often to be thought Jacob wrestled with an angel, the story itself makes the startling claim that it is very God with whom he wrestled.

Jacob named the place "Peniel" (the face of God); for he said, *"I have seen God face to face, and my life is spared."* Genesis 32:30

Though God is not a man, God, we presume, may take whatever form fits the occasion. Perhaps though, this account is merely a literary way of saying Jacob wrestled with his conscience, something perhaps he had not really done before. And even now, it is only because he is filled with fear. In that wrestling, it says he prevailed. What does that mean? Who can wrestle with God and prevail? There was a Broadway Gospel Musical that toured a few years ago called, *"Your Arm's Too Short to Box With God."* It seems an obvious truth, so how did Jacob prevail? Perhaps it means that he survived this encounter with himself. Perhaps it means that at last, with no way around, no way to rationalize what he had done, this opportunist comes face to face with himself, comes face to face with the man of vaulting ambition, the manipulator, the exploiter, the abuser. Can Jacob see himself, see what he has done, and deny what he sees, what he knows? He prevails in that wrestling with his conscience he obtains the truth, the truth of himself, who he is and what he has done. He sees it, accepts it in his heart and is changed. He sees God face to face, and yet his life is spared. He is changed, but his very body is marked by his ordeal. His stride is turned into a limp. His pride is bent. He is humbled at last.

As the dawn comes Jacob clings to the one with whom he has wrestled demanding a blessing. And what is the meaning of that? What blessing? Is it like that blessing, the birthright, gained by deception, that his father Isaac had given him? Is it not audacious to ask that what he had gained by deceit he should be allowed to keep? Does the thief when caught get to keep what he has stolen. The one with whom Jacob has wrestled asks him his name. He answers, "Jacob." And the one with whom he has wrestled tells him that henceforth is name will be, "Israel." It is God who gives him his name because only God can give him a new name signifying a new man, a new nature, a changed heart. The person he was, Jacob, is gone, but what now is his life to be? Where to from here? Will Esau's great entourage overtake all of his own and claim all that Jacob had connived to take from him? Will his family be taken captive? his beloved Rachel? his children? Joseph? Will all that his ambition has got him be taken now from him, perhaps even his life? Jacob had taken advantage of his brother's less aggressive, less ambitious nature, to empower himself. Now he cannot go forward, cannot claim his destiny, without encountering Esau. He trembles for fear of what he knows would be his brother's righteous anger. In the morning his great dread is turned unexpectedly to exquisite joy from a source he never imagined. It comes remarkably, incredibly, from the very one he so greatly feared, his brother Esau.

And Jacob lifted up his eyes and looked and behold Esau was coming with four hundred men. So he divided the children among Leah and Rachael and the two maids. And he put the maids with their children in front, then Leah with her children, and Rachael and Joseph last of all. He himself went before them, bowing himself to the ground seven times, until he came near to his brother. But Esau ran to meet him, and embraced him, and fell on his neck, and kissed him, and they wept. Genesis 33:1-4

As one of the two great stories of reconciliation in the Old Testament, the meeting of Jacob and Esau rivals only that one when Jacob's own son, Joseph, Prince of Egypt, discloses himself to his brothers. Is Joseph inspired - able - to forgive his brothers because he saw and remembers how his uncle Esau forgave his father Jacob? Analogies are not perfect, but this story, I believe fits what is now happening. Through a long night, which may be far from over, the Church has wrestled with God because it has taken advantage of her gay brothers and sisters nature to claim the birthright and to empower herself. The effect has been to cast this brother and sister out. Yet now that one is there, and as much as it despises the predicament, there is no way forward for the Church to be the Church without coming face to face with that brother and sister. The Church dreads that real encounter. God would perhaps let her go to suffer the consequences, further decline and mounting irrelevance, of the choices she has made, but she clings to God to save her from the outcome of what she has done.

Denominations debate and struggle over some change in the policy or constitution regarding the inclusion of gays. So far most of them have stubbornly resisted real change. But all of this does not yet come near the heart of the matter. The deeper thing is that among the many there is yet very little recognition and regret, and therefore no real repentance for what it has done, and taught others to do. But it is from the heart that real change must come. Most of the Church has not yet let go of its pride on this, has not yet been humbled, has not yet been touched, put out of joint, in her body.

Much of the Church is still trying only to find a way around this one it fears to meet face to face. It does not see it, of course. It is still righteous in its own eyes. Without empathy, how can you know the pain you have caused? Yet that which the Church lacks, though it does not even know its own emptiness, will likely come, remarkably, incredibly, from the very one whose righteous anger it so greatly fears. While the Church stands frozen in that fear of the one it has wronged, it may find that it is that gay brother and sister who will be first to offer their embrace. Driven out, like Esau, many gays have made a life and a family for themselves. They have prospered and many of them have become whole. Some of them have even found their own way to God. It is not they who need absolution from the Church. It is the Church, much of it, that is wretched, miserable, and needy, because of how it has treated this brother and sister.

In the later days, when the healing has come, and I do believe someday it will come, we may observe that the mark of this struggle and the shame of it has made this body, at last, a more just, more compassionate, and a more humble one. It will have recovered the knowledge that what God really requires of us is not our pretensions to purity, but to *"seek justice, love kindness, and to walk humbly with our God."* When it has moved beyond mere forbearance, and past previous intolerance, to a true embrace of gay and lesbian persons, it can begin to claim fully its mission and its destiny, which has been held somewhat hostage by its fears. When the Church no longer despises part of its own body it will be more visibly the Body of Christ. We will come to know, gay or straight - whatever our nature, that God's grace is true grace, though abominable to some, it is always amazing.

NOTES

Chapter 2

p. 31 "Eyes of Tammy Faye"
2000 documentary film of Tammy Faye Bakker Messer, directed by Fenton Bailey.

p. 42 Dobson's "Focus On The Family"
This conservative Christian organization was founded 1977 in Colorado Springs, Colorado, by James Dobson, psychologist.

Chapter 3

p. 47 "Scared to Death"
A 1993 video of interviews with gay men coping with societal responses to their sexual orientation. Produced by the Lazarus Project, West Hollywood Presbyterian Church, West Hollywood, CA

p. 48 "Southern Baptist Sissies"
A play in two acts, by Del Shores, 2000. Originally produced at The Zephyr Theatre, West Hollywood, CA

pp. 55-57 Testimonials re: "reparative therapy"
Founded in Rochester, N.Y. in 1996 "One by One" is an organization associated with the United Presbyterian Church U.S.A.

Chapter 4

pp. 59-61 "All In the Family" episode "Two's a Crowd"

episode 172, aired February 12, 1978.

p. 64 "A Sleep of Prisoners"
A Sleep Of Prisoners was published in 1951, and first performed at St Thomas' church in Regent Street, London, in 1951. Fry's interest was in writing a play to illustrate that differences and conflicts between people "springing often...from the outward amour, the facades behind which we hide our spirits." Four male actors play prisoners of war detained in a church turned prison camp, stripped bare except for the pulpit and four wooden beds. By day we see the surface of the men—the outward behaviors and characteristics which distinguish them, one from the other. By night, they sleep and fold into each others' dreams. Each one dreams of himself and the other three as larger than life biblical characters—Cain and Abel, Absalom, David and Joab, Abraham and Isaac, and finally Sadrac, Mesak, and Abendego—four dream stories of relationships laced with trauma, passion, faith, and their accompanying vicissitudes of deception, betrayal, love, loyalty, and redemption.

p. 67. "Geraldine" was a character created by comedian Flip Wilson seen on "The Flip Wilson Show" an NBC series broadcast Sept. 1970 to June 1974, directed by Bob Henry.

Chapter 5

p. 82 play "JB"
"J.B." is a 1958 play written in free verse by American playwright and poet Archibald MacLeish, and is a modern retelling of the story of the biblical figure Job.

p. 86 Zulu "nkul unkulu"
Unkulunkulu is the creator god and great ancestral spirit of the Zulu people. Unkulunkulu is believed to have grown on a reed in the mythical swamp of Uhlanga. In the isiZulu language, the name means "the very great/high one."

p. 86 "The Creation" an oratorio
This is part of a larger work called "God's Trombones: Seven Negro Sermons in verse," a 1927 book of poems by James Weldon Johnson patterned after traditional African-American religious oratory. African-American scholars Henry Louis Gates and Cornel West have identified the collection as one of Johnson's two most notable works.

p. 88 "A Sleep of Prisoners" See note from chapter 4.

Chapter 6

p. 91 "Porgy and Bess"
Porgy and Bess is an opera, first performed in 1935, with music by George Gershwin, libretto by DuBose Heyward, and lyrics by Ira Gershwin and DuBose Heyward.

p. 93 "Stranger at the Gate"
This is an autobiographical book by Mel White (April 1995) Penguin Group (USA). Coming from an evangelical background, this book has been influential in the gay liberation movement. Mel White is also the founder of "Soul Force" an advocacy organization for homosexual persons.

p. 95 "Boswell, etc.

John Boswell, "Same-Sex Unions in Premodern Europe" Boswell, now deceased, was the past chairman of Yale's history department, was gay and a convert to Catholicism. He resided in New Haven with his partner. This book has been widely acclaimed. Boswell contends that during the Middle Ages Catholic and Orthodox churches developed liturgical rites for solemnizing unions between pairs of males. If the thesis of the book is correct, the clear implication is that homosexual relationships, even those with an erotic aspect, have not always been regarded by Christians as sinful. Indeed, they may have been viewed at times as exemplary of Christian virtue. A further implication is that the current position of the Catholic and Orthodox churches, that homosexual activity is gravely sinful, may be a cultural accretion that does not have its roots in authentic Christian belief.

Most Christians, even those in sympathy with Boswell, will find his claims surprising. However, his reputation, as holder of the Griswold Chair in History at Yale, and the apparent weight of his evidence have impressed many readers. His research seems to be meticulously thorough, and his text is copiously supplemented with notes documenting often obscure sources in Greek, Latin, Russian, Hebrew, Arabic, Serbian, French, German and various other languages. Boswell took care to footnote everything. It is true that this might have been an attempt to overwhelm any opponent, but a momentary consideration of the context removes such a possibility: if Boswell had written without footnotes we all know that he would have been dismissed out of hand.

John J. McNeill, S.J. "The Church and the Homosexual" Beacon Press, 1993, original publication 1976. The author is a priest and psychotherapist.

Daniel A. Helminiak, 'What the Bible Really Says About Homosexuality" Alamo Square Press 2000. Psychology Professor. Daniel A. Helminiak, holds a Ph.D. in systematic theology from Boston College and Andover Newton Theological School, and a Ph.D. in educational psychology from The University of Texas at Austin. He is also currently a professor at the University of West Georgia.

Walter Wink, "Biblical Perspectives on Homosexuality" Walter Wink Books 1999, Walter Wink, a Methodist, is Emeritus Professor of Biblical Interpretation, Auburn Theological Seminary, New York City. An earlier version of this article appeared in the Christian Century Magazine. ©1979, Scripture quotes are from the NRSV unless otherwise noted. Reprinted by permission. Revised version © by Walter Wink. This article is available as a 16-page booklet from Fellowship Books Box 271, Nyack NY 10960.

William Countryman, "Dirt, Sex, and Greed: Sexual Ethics in the New Testament and Their Implications for Today" Minneapolis: Augsburg-Fortress Press 1988. William Countryman is professor of Religion at Pacific School of Religion, Berkeley, CA.

Jack Rogers, "Jesus, The Bible, and Homosexuality: Explode the Myths, Heal the Church" Westminster John Knox Press; Louisville, KY, 2006. The author was Moderator of the 213th (2001) General Assembly of The United Presbyterian Church USA . Jack Rogers has been a Professor at Fuller Seminary, and more recently was the President (southern campus) of The San Francisco Theological Seminary.

Chapter 7

   p. 110 "On The Road"
On the Road is a novel by American writer Jack Kerouac, published in 1957 by Viking Press.

   p. 111 "His Eye Is on the Sparrow"
"His Eye Is on the Sparrow" is a Gospel hymn. Although today it is a staple of African-American worship services, the song was originally written in 1905 by two white songwriters, lyricist Civilla D. Martin and composer Charles H. Gabriel. The song is most associated with actress-singer Ethel Waters who used the title for her autobiography.

   p.117 Lily Tomlin "The Search for Signs of Intelligent Life in the Universe (1991) "- was written by Jane Wagner and directed by John Bailey. Lily Tomlin won the 1986 Tony Award (NYC) for best actress in a drama.

   p. 118 & p.181 Brokeback Mountain
Brokeback Mountain is a 2005 romantic drama film directed by Ang Lee. It is a film adaptation of the 1997 short story of the same name by Annie Proulx. The film stars Jake Gyllenhaal and Heath Ledger as young cowboys named Jack Twist and Ennis Del Mar. Each of them is hired to corral sheep on the title location and they soon bond very closely. Their platonic relationship explodes into a physical one, but eventually the two are separated when their job comes to an end. Although the two follow different life paths -- one becoming a father of two and the other marrying into a successful business -- they have a reunion years later. Each is affected profoundly by the rekindling of

their old feelings for each other. Those feelings lead each to consider what continuing their hidden relationship would cost them. The screenplay was written by Pulitzer Prize-winning author Larry McMurtry and Diana Ossana.

p. 120 Sleep of Prisoners - see notes under Chapter 4

p.123 Vatican - homosexuality "inheretly disordered" Issued on October 31, 1986, by then Cardinal Joseph Ratzinger (now Pope Benedict XVI) prefect of the Congregation of the Doctrine of Faith, it expressed traditional teachings in very harsh and uncompromising language. According to his "Letter to the Bishops of the Catholic Church on the Pastoral Care of Homosexual Persons," *"Although the particular inclination of the homosexual person is not a sin, it is a more or less strong tendency ordered toward an intrinsic moral evil; thus the inclination itself must be seen as an objective disorder...* The key here is the phrase "objective disorder" — the Vatican had not used such language before and it outraged many. Pope Benedict was telling people that even if homosexuality is not freely chosen by each individual, it is nevertheless *inherently* and objectively wrong. It's not merely that homosexual activity is wrong, but homosexuality itself — the orientation of being emotionally, psychologically, and physically attracted to members of the same sex — that is objectively wrong. Not a "sin," but still wrong.

Chapter 8

p. 131-132 Brothers Karamazov
"The Brothers Karamazov" is the final novel by the Russian author Fyodor Dostoyevsky. Dostoyevsky spent nearly two years writing The Brothers Karamazov, which

was published as a serial in The Russian Messenger and completed in November 1880. Dostoyevsky intended it to be the first part in an epic story titled "The Life of a Great Sinner," but he died less than four months after its publication.

p. 133 The Outsider

"The Outsider" is a non-fiction book by Colin Wilson first published in 1956. Through the works and lives of various artists - including H. G. Wells (Mind at the End of its Tether), Franz Kafka, Albert Camus, Jean-Paul Sartre, T. S. Eliot, Ernest Hemingway, Harley Granville-Barker (The Secret Life), Hermann Hesse, T. E. Lawrence, Vincent Van Gogh, Vaslav Nijinsky, George Bernard Shaw, William Blake, Friedrich Nietzsche, Fyodor Dostoevsky and G. I. Gurdjieff - Wilson explores the psyche of the Outsider, his effect on society, and society's effect on him. Wilson wrote "The Outsider" in the Reading Room of the British Museum, and during this period was living in a sleeping bag on Hampstead Heath.

p. 134 Sounds of Silence

"The Sounds of Silence" is the song that propelled the 1960s folk music duo Simon & Garfunkel to popularity. It was written in February 1964 by Paul Simon in the aftermath of the 1963 assassination of John F. Kennedy. An initial version preferred by the band was remixed and sweetened, and has become known as "the quintessential folk rock release". In the U.S., it was the duo's second most popular hit after "Bridge Over Troubled Water."

p.140 "What Evangelicals Believe"

This book by David Allan Hubbard was published in 1991 by Fuller Seminary Press. Hubbard was at that time President of the seminary.

Chapter 9

p.144 All in the Family

"All in the Family" is an American sitcom that was originally broadcast on the CBS television network from January 12, 1971 to April 8, 1979. In September 1979, a new show, "Archie Bunker's Place," picked up where "All in the Family" had ended. This sitcom lasted another four years, ending its run in 1983.

Produced by Norman Lear, it was based on the British television comedy series "Till Death Us Do Part." The show broke ground in its depiction of issues previously considered unsuitable for U.S. network television comedy, such as racism, homosexuality, women's liberation, rape, miscarriage, abortion, breast cancer, the Vietnam War, menopause, and impotence.

p. 146 The Full Monty

"The Full Monty" is a 1997 British comedy film directed by Peter Cattaneo, starring Robert Carlyle, Mark Addy, William Snape, Steve Huison, Tom Wilkinson, Paul Barber, and Hugo Speer. The screenplay was written by Simon Beaufoy. The film is set in Sheffield, England. The film was later turned into a stage production set in Buffalo, New York.

p.149 Promisekeepers

"Promisekeepers" is an international conservative Christian organization for men. While it originated in the United States, it is now world-wide. It was founded in 1990 by Bill McCartney, the controversial and outspoken ex-coach of the University of Colorado football team.

p.151-152 Films: "Strawberry & Chocolate" & "Big Eden"

"Strawberry and Chocolate" (1994) This Cuban film tells the story of Diego, a cultivated, homosexual and skeptical young man, falls in love with a young heterosexual communist full of prejudices and doctrinary ideas, Directors: Tomás Gutiérrez Alea, Juan Carlos Tabío Writers: Senel Paz (screenplay), Senel Paz (story) Stars: Jorge Perugorría, Vladimir Cruz and Mirta Ibarra.

"Big Eden" (2000) is a gay-themed romantic drama film written and directed by Thomas Bezucha. The film stars Arye Gross as Henry Hart, a successful gay artist from New York City who returns to his rural hometown in Montana to care for his ailing grandfather. Henry is welcomed back by the townsfolk, all of whom are aware of his sexuality and are highly accepting and even supportive towards him (the film's plot and dialogue notably has a complete absence of homophobic content). However, during the months he stays in the town, Henry is forced to confront his unresolved feelings for his high school friend Dean Stewart (Tim DeKay), while simultaneously beginning to fall in love with Pike Dexter (Eric Schweig), the shy Native American owner of the town's general store.

Chapter 10

p. 156 Matthew Shepherd

Matthew Wayne Shepard (December 1, 1976 – October 12, 1998) was a student at the University of Wyoming who was tortured and murdered near Laramie, Wyoming, in October 1998. He was attacked on the night of October 6–7, and died at Poudre Valley Hospital in Fort Collins, Colorado, on October 12 from severe head injuries.

During the trial, witnesses stated that Shepard was targeted because of his sexual orientation. Shepard's murder brought national and international attention to the contention of hate crime legislation at the state and federal levels.

In 2009, his mother Judy Shepard authored a book "The Meaning of Matthew: My Son's Murder in Laramie, and a World Transformed." On October 22, 2009, the United States Congress passed the Matthew Shepard and James Byrd, Jr. Hate Crimes Prevention Act (Matthew Shepard Act for short), and on October 28, 2009, President Obama signed the legislation into law.

   p. 160 "Strictly Ballroom"
Strictly Ballroom is a 1992 Australian romantic comedy film directed and co-written by Baz Luhrmann and produced by M&A Productions.

   p. 164 American Gothic, painting by Grant Wood

Wood's best known work is his 1930 painting "American Gothic," which is also one of the most famous paintings in American art and one of the few images to reach the status of universally recognized cultural icon, comparable to Leonardo da Vinci's "Mona Lisa" and Edvard Munch's "The Scream." It was first exhibited in 1930 at the Art Institute of Chicago, where it is still located. Art critics who had favorable opinions about the painting, such as Gertrude Stein and Christopher Morley, assumed the painting was meant to be a satire of repression and narrow-mindedness of rural small-town life. It was seen as part of the trend toward increasingly critical depictions of rural America, along the lines of Sherwood Anderson's 1919 "Winesburg, Ohio," Sinclair Lewis' 1920 "Main Street," and Carl Van Vechten's "The Tattooed Countess" in literature. Wood rejected this reading of it. With the onset of the Great Depression, it came to be seen as a depiction of steadfast American pioneer spirit. Another reading is that it is an ambiguous fusion of reverence and parody. Wood's inspiration came from Eldon, southern Iowa, where a cottage designed in the Gothic Revival style with an upper window in the shape of a medieval pointed arch, provided the background and also the painting's title. Wood decided to paint the house along with "the kind of people I fancied should live in that house." The painting shows a farmer standing beside his spinster daughter, figures modeled by the artist's dentist and sister, Nan (1900–1990). The dentist, Dr. Byron McKeeby (1867–1950) was from Cedar Rapids, Iowa. The woman is dressed in a colonial print apron mimicking 19th century Americana and the couple are in the traditional roles of men and women, the man's pitchfork symbolizing hard labor.The compositional severity and detailed technique derive from Northern Renaissance paintings, which Grant had looked at during three visits to Europe; after this he became increasingly aware of the Midwest's own legacy, which also informs the work. It is a key image of Regionalism.

p. 166 "Seinfeld" episode

"The Outing" is the fifty-seventh episode of the sitcom "Seinfeld." It is the 17th episode of the fourth season, and first aired on February 11, 1993. The line "... Not that there's anything wrong with that" has become a popular phrase among fans.

    p.168-169 June 25, 1970.
Janis Joplin performs "Get It While You Can" live on the Dick Cavett Show, followed by the interview about her forthcoming return to her hometown, Port Arthur, Texas.

    p. 169 movie "The Rose"
"The Rose" (1979): Loosely based on the life of iconic rocker Janis Joplin, the film follows a superstar called The Rose on her last tour when she returned to her hometown. It was written by Bill Kerby, and Bo Goldman from a story by Bill Kerby, and directed by Mark Rydell.

    p. 169-120 The Stonewall Rebellion
Stonewall riots were a series of spontaneous, violent demonstrations against a police raid that took place in the early morning hours of June 28, 1969, at the Stonewall Inn, in the Greenwich Village neighborhood of New York City. They are frequently cited as the first instance in American history when people in the homosexual community fought back against a government-sponsored system that persecuted sexual minorities, and they have become the defining event that marked the start of the gay rights movement in the United States and around the world.

Chapter 11

    p.174 "All In the Family" episode 65 - Archie and the Kiss 10/6/73. See note under chapter 4.

p. 183 "Tristan and Isuelt" and Abelard and Heloise
The legend of Tristan and Isuelt is an influential romance and tragedy, retold in numerous sources with as many variations. The tragic story is of the adulterous love between the Cornish knight Tristan (Tristram) and the Irish princess Isuelt (Isolde, Yseult, etc.). The narrative predates and most likely influenced the Arthurian romance of Lancelot and Guinevere, and has had a substantial impact on Western art, the idea of romantic love and literature since it first appeared in the 12th century. While the details of the story differ from one author to another, the overall plot structure remains much the same.

Peter Abelard (English pronunciation) 1079 – April 21, 1142, was a medieval French scholastic philosopher, theologian and preeminent logician. The story of his affair with and love for Héloïse has become legendary. The Chambers Biographical Dictionary describes him as "the keenest thinker and boldest theologian of the 12th Century. Living within the precincts of Notre-Dame, under the care of her uncle, the canon Fulbert, was Héloïse. She was remarkable for her knowledge of classical letters, which extended beyond Latin to Greek and Hebrew. Abélard sought a place in Fulbert's house, and then seduced Héloïse. The affair interfered with his career, and Abélard himself boasted of his conquest. Once Fulbert found out, they were separated, but met in secret. Héloïse became pregnant and was sent by Abélard to Brittany, where she gave birth to a son she named Astrolabe after the instrument. To appease Fulbert, Abélard proposed a secret marriage in order not to mar his career prospects. Héloïse initially opposed it, but the couple married. When Fulbert publicly disclosed the marriage, and Héloïse denied it, she went to the convent of Argenteuil at Abélard's urging. Fulbert, believing that Abélard wanted to be rid of Héloïse, had him castrated, effectively ending Abélard's romantic career. Héloïse was forced to become a nun. Héloïse sent letters to Abélard, questioning why she must submit to a religious life for which she had no calling.

p. 187 "Queer as Folk"
This TV drama ran from 2000 through 2005 depicting the lives, loves, and relationships of a group of gay friends living in Pittsburgh, Pennsylvania. Directors: Michael DeCarlo, John Fawcett, and 6 more credits »Writers: Doug Guinan (episodes), Richard Kramer (episodes), and 3 more credits. Stars: Gale Harold, Hal Sparks and Randy Harrison.

p. 189 "The Iceman Cometh"
"The Iceman Cometh" is a play written by American playwright Eugene O'Neill in 1939. First published in 1940 the play premiered on Broadway at the Martin Beck Theatre.

Chapter 12

p. 192 "The Cost of Discipleship"
The Cost of Discipleship is a book by the German Theologian Dietrich Bonhoeffer, considered a classic of Christian thought. The original German title is simply Nachfolge (Discipleship). It is centered around an exposition of the Sermon on the Mount, in which Bonhoeffer spells out what he believes it means to follow Christ. It was first published in 1937, when the rise of the Nazi regime was underway in Germany and against this background Bonhoeffer's theology of costly discipleship developed, which ultimately led to his execution by hanging ordered by Heinrich Himler during the last days of the Nazi regime.. "cheap *grace is the preaching of forgiveness without requiring repentance, baptism without*

church discipline, Communion without confession. Cheap grace is grace without discipleship, grace without the cross, grace without Jesus Christ."

p. 193 "Drinking the Water" Steve Peterson
This song is from "Let Freedom Ring!" a liberation collection, words and music by Steve Peterson. Peterson's voice sings out in memory of James Byrd, Jr. an African-American man who was dragged to death behind a pickup truck, and to Matthew Shepherd, a young gay man beaten beyond recognition, tied to a fence and left to die. This collection "Let Freedom Ring" was written for all victims of hate crimes. Available through Harmony Grove Music, P.O. Box 19214, Seattle, WA 9819

p. 194 "Young Man Luther"
Erik H. Erikson (American psychoanalyst) In "Young Man Luther " (1958), combined his interest in history and psychoanalytic theory to examine how Martin Luther was able to break with the existing religious establishment to create a new way of looking at the world. Gandhi's "Truth on the Origins of Militant Nonviolence" (1969) also was a psychohistory.

p. 200 Wm Stringfellow "My People Is the Enemy"
Frank William Stringfellow (April 26, 1928 – March 2, 1985) was an American lay theologian. My People Is the Enemy, New York, NY: Holt, Rinehart and Winston, was published in 1964. Just a few short years later, Stringfellow gained a reputation as a strident critic of the social, military and economic policies of the U.S. and as a tireless advocate for racial and social justice. That justice, he declared, could be realized only if it were pursued according to a serious understanding of the Bible and the Christian faith.

p. 202-203 "Peter and the Wolf"
Peter and the Wolf (Russian), Op. 67, is a composition written by Sergei Prokofiev in 1936 in the USSR. It is a children's story (with both ...Peter and the Wolf (disambiguation) - Peter and the Wolf (1946 film) an animated dramatization of the 1936 musical composition by Sergei Prokofiev, produced by Walt Disney, with Sterling Holloway providing the voice of the narrator. It was originally released theatrically in 1946 as a segment in Make Mine Music. It was re-issued the following year accompanying a re-issue of Fantasia (as a short subject before the film), then released separately on home video in the 1990s.

p. 210 Mark Thompson's "Gay Soul"
Gay & Lesbian › Biographies & Memoirs Amazon. com: Gay Soul: Finding the Heart of Gay Spirit and Nature with Sixteen Writers, Healers, Teachers : Mark Thompson - 1994.

Chapter 13

p. 213 Steve Peterson, see note under chapter 12

p. 221 hymn "Farther Along"
The story goes that Rev. W. A. Fletcher, an itinerant preacher, wrote the lyrics while traveling on a train to the Indian Territories near the end of 1911, apparently to reflect his depression at knowing he would not be with his wife for the approaching birth of his first child as he felt obliged to carry out his ministry far from home. The theme is that wicked people seem to prosper whereas the righteous Christian often has to suffer, but that the apparent injustice will all be explained when we get to Heaven. He happened

to be sitting next to J. R. Baxter, a gospel music promoter who liked the lyrics and paid Fletcher for them. He then had them put to music and it became a popular Southern gospel song: *"Farther along we'll know more about it, farther along we'll understand why."* There are several contradictory claims for the authorship of this song. One is the W. A. Fletcher version, another is that this gospel song is an African American spiritual of unknown origin.

p. 223-224 "Your Arm's Too Short To Box With God" Produced by Frankie Hewitt and the Shubert Organization, it opened December 1976, at Broadway's Lyceum Theatre in NewYork City. It Moved to the Eugene O'Neill theatre in November 1977 and closed January 1, 1978, after 429 performances. "Your Arm's Too Short To Box With God" is a soaring celebration in song and dance based on the Biblical Book of Matthew, with music and lyrics by Alex Bradford and a book by Vinnette Carroll, who also directed. Micki Grant was credited for "additional music and lyrics."

Made in the USA
Charleston, SC
04 August 2012